DATE DUE

	OCT 27 2008		

Demco, Inc. 38-293

WITH A BANJO
ON MY KNEE

WITH A BANJO ON MY KNEE

A Musical Journey From Slavery to Freedom

BY DR. REX M. ELLIS

Cover ©: Hampton University Museum, Hampton, VA ("The Banjo Lesson", by Henry Ossawa Tanner, oil on canvas, 1893.

Photographs ©: Archive Photos: 65 (American Stock), 73 (Blank Archives), 68, 69, 71, 112, 115 (Frank Driggs), 20, 25, 31, 34, 35, 39, 95; Brown Brothers: 53, 54, 90, 97; Brown University Library: 93; Corbis-Bettmann: 118 (UPI), 43, 56, 82; Culver Pictures: 13, 29, 77, 78, 81, 84; Frank Driggs Collection: 116 (Ray Flerlage), 12, 55, 87, 99, 107; Schomburg Center for Research in Black Culture, Photographs and Prints Division, New York Public Library: 57 (Helen Armstead-Johnson Photograph Collection, photo by Dalbey), 14 (V.G. Schreck).

Interior design by Elizabeth Helmetsie

Library of Congress Cataloging-in-Publication Data
Ellis, Rex M., 1951–
    With a Banjo on My Knee: A Musical Journey From Slavery to Freedom/by Rex M. Ellis
        p. cm.
    Includes bibliographical references and index.
    ISBN 0-531-11747-2
        1. Banjoists—United States—Biography—Juvenile literature. 2. Afro-American Musicians—Biography—Juvenile literature. [1. Banjo. 2. Banjoists. 3. Afro-Americans—Biography.] I. Title.
    ML399.E45 2001
    787.898908996073—dc21   00-033035

For Paulette, Amber, Aaron,
and all those African-American banjo players
who made music that contributed to
the unity of our community.

Preface

This book is meant to explore the many ways being black in America affected the music of African-Americans and particularly the role played by the banjo. What can we learn about the times in which these musicians lived? How did those times affect our current ideas of what it means to be black in America? Why did these musicians begin playing the banjo in the first place? How did it influence their lives? What were the results of the sacrifices and choices they made to pursue the instrument? How did it change them as people? How did it affect their families and their communities? How did the times in which they lived contribute to, or hinder their success? What were their aspirations, their dreams, and their hopes? Was the banjo a hobby, an occupation, an all-consuming passion, or just a passing fancy that turned into much more over time? How did it affect the other traditional roles they were expected to play as fathers, mothers, sisters, brothers, children, husbands, wives, and workers? Was the banjo and the desire to play it, a balance that allowed all their life experiences to work in harmony, or did it overshadow everything? These are the questions I will explore.

Musicians, scholars, historians, folklorists, and others have been writing about the banjo and its African roots for more than thirty years. Because of this research, most people who play, or spend lots of time with people who play the banjo, know that this musical instrument's roots stretch back to Africa.

In the last twenty years or so, there has been renewed interest in the banjo, particularly its connections to African and African-American history and culture. This curiosity has produced new research that has helped students, scholars, and historians gain a greater understanding of the banjo's journey from Africa to America. It has also done a great deal to correct the long-held belief that the banjo originated in the Appalachian region of North America. We now know that the banjo is not connected exclusively to rural white Southerners from Appalachia, or anywhere else, even though that is probably where you still see it most. Research has taught us that the banjo has roots that reach back to the Senegambia region of West Africa.[1]

Quite a bit has already been said about the songs, styles of playing, construction, and adaptations of the banjo. We also know something of banjo players and how their playing of the instrument contributed to our knowledge of the music, styles of playing, and the customs that still survive today.

However, far less has been said that helps us understand the context for how the music, the instrument, and those who played it from the beginning were influenced by the social, political, and economic realities of their day. There has been no in-depth discussion of the musicians, the world they lived in, and how their world-view influences our notions of culture, race, and American identity.

The banjo, as an instrument, has undergone a great deal of change. It has not been a part of the African-American community since the first quarter of the twentieth century. Today, budding African-American musicians pick up the guitar in households all across America, but not the banjo. In fact, many elders who played the banjo in their youth, have hidden or concealed that fact instead of discussing it openly. For most of them, it is not an instrument that engenders pride.

Older African-Americans (those above fifty) may remember the popularity of the banjo in the early twentieth century because, prior to the popularization of the guitar, banjos were the stringed rhythm instrument of choice. It was briefly liberated from the minstrel stage of the nineteenth century and went uptown to jazz clubs and concert stages around the world. Many older Americans can still recall relatives, friends, and community members who played the instrument. But for too many of these people, it is not a memory that is cherished. Some people can remember entertainment that featured or included the banjo—radio shows, local fairs, novelty acts, national headliners, performances on concert stages and in formal music halls. However, the memory has faded, or been replaced by more contemporary and popular views of what is "acceptable." Unfortunately, in the African-American community, that leaves out the banjo.

Most African-Americans who play the banjo currently do so as a result of coaxing from an increasing number of scholars. Most of these scholars are not members of the community they seek to "honor," but who have cajoled, encouraged, and convinced African-American banjo players that the instrument is indeed important and significant.[2]

In order to revive and chronicle the black banjo tradition, many of these scholars and their associates have produced compact discs, tapes, anthologies, and all types of publications. Their research has made them authorities, and many have enjoyed serving as spokespeople for that tradition. In their efforts to collect and preserve the banjo's true history, they have given a great deal of attention to the folk music tradition (i.e., music created in informal settings by musicians with little or no formal training). However, their efforts have not resulted in folk music's acceptance in the African-American community. It is still seen as too one-dimensional, nostalgic, self-serving, insignificant, and patronizing. In all honesty, however, if the research of these contemporary scholars had not taken place, much of what is understood about the banjo and its roots would not be known today.

The banjo was part of a culture in transition. As Africans and African-Americans moved from slavery to freedom, so did their musical expression. This movement represented a unique social and cultural world that changed and evolved over time. Like the rise and decline of ragtime, the banjo became a victim of its time, especially within the black community.

Space will not allow a discussion of the influences of the banjo relating to the Caribbean, or Central and South American communities. Yet it must be mentioned that African musical roots, relating to the banjo, survive in a number of these communities as well.

The Caribbean climate allowed for a more identifiable and specific connection to Africa. Because of the strictures of slavery, the average life span of Africans in the Caribbean was six to ten years. The harsh treatment of enslaved women resulted in them being sterile. This fact had a negative impact on Africans being able to reproduce themselves. So slave owners returned to Africa more frequently than they did in North America, especially in the seventeenth century, to enslave more Africans. They were brought to these islands to work in the sugar plantations that existed on many islands in the Caribbean. This constant importation of new Africans to the Caribbean resulted in them having a more consistent and direct connection to their native land. As a result, their cultural expressions, beliefs, and understanding of the world was more closely linked to their "African" ancestry than their experience as new Americans.

These communities and their experiences are important in understanding the development of early North American musical influences, but beyond the scope of this book. It is my hope that this book will encourage further investigation relating to the cultural evolution of these areas, and their connection to the North American banjo tradition within the African-American community.

My own discovery of the banjo and its significance to the African-American community has been a unique journey. It began while I was working at Colonial Williamsburg in the 1970s and 1980s. During those years, I frequently discovered documents, runaway ads, diary accounts, letters, and inventories that mentioned the banjo in connection with Africans and African-Americans. In fact, the banjo was second only to the fiddle as an instrument played by enslaved Africans. These documents also helped me understand the importance and popularity of music to the black community. The more I encountered evidence about the banjo, the more it fueled my desire to share its history with others who had no clue of its heritage.

As I began thinking of ways to present this new information to the public, I realized that I needed to learn how to play the thing. A friend at Colonial Williamsburg suggested I contact Dave Barr, a banjo player and veterinarian, who also had a passion for the instrument and its history. It was Dave who opened the floodgates of my imagination and introduced me to Bob Zentz, who ran a store in Virginia Beach, Virginia, called "Ramblin Conrads," and it was Bob who sold me my first banjo. Between healing sick dogs and cats, Dave worked with me and after awhile we both realized that I had to branch out even further. He suggested I attend the Augusta Heritage Festival in Elkins, West Virginia, where I took my first formal banjo lesson in 1989. For five days, I ate with, slept with, and spent every waking hour strumming on my new banjo. I was not only immersed with the instrument, but most of the people who surrounded me were also banjo players. It was also at Elkins where I first met and talked with African-American folk musicians, such as Howard Armstrong, John Jackson, Nat Reese, John Cephus, and Phil Wiggins.

From there the world of the banjo, and banjo players, opened to include new friends and wonderful banjo players, such as Joe Herrmann, Tony Ellis,

Reed Martin, Dwight Diller, and Mike Seegar. Their knowledge, love of the instrument, and willingness to befriend and share their knowledge with me has been integral to my understanding. People whose research and scholarship I have grown to respect and depend on—Dena Epstein, Robert Winans, Cece Conway, Karen Linn, Eileen Southern, Howard Sackler, and Phillip Gura—have helped me immeasurably through this process. A host of new friends, colleagues, and well-wishers such as Jerry Milnes, John Jackson, Sule Greg Wilson, Selasse Damasie, Baba Jemo Kuyata, Scott Odell, and Otis Taylor have helped in ways they are not aware of. I am also grateful to readers and advisors at the Smithsonian. Some of these colleagues are John Hasse, Gary Sturm, Howard Bass, and Stacey Kluck.

Special thanks are given, as well, to the banjo players whose history and contributions to the African-American banjo tradition have inspired this book.

Finally, my work would not have taken place without the constant support, love, encouragement, and goading of my family. My wife Paulette has been my best friend, my careful critic, and my chief supporter. My daughter, Amber, who is the quintessential teenager, has provided respites of reality and humor when I least expected them; and my son Aaron (who has left the roost and begun his own journey into the heady ranks of higher education) has quietly and calmly reminded me that this too was possible and necessary to do. To all of them go my thanks and my gratitude. I am who they have helped me be.

Rex Marshall Ellis
August 2000

Table of Contents

*This photo, taken in 1905, shows an
elderly banjo player. The photographer captured the
hard life of a traveling minstrel.*

Introduction

S o what is the deal with this banjo thing? Why is the cultural evolution of the banjo and its existence in the African-American community so important? The banjo has made a significant contribution to American music in general. Much of that contribution has been the result of African and African-American influences. The particular contribution of African-Americans to the music scene is directly related to their enslavement in America.

We cannot talk about African-American music without talking about slavery and its influence. It was enslavement that fashioned their musical experience and provided an escape from the horrors of slavery. As W. E. B. Du Bois, the famous African-American scholar said, ". . . these songs are the articulate message of the slave to the world . . . they are the music of an unhappy people, of the children of disappointment; they tell of death and suffering, and unvoiced longing toward a truer world, of misty wanderings and hidden ways."[3] African-American musical expression began as a result of their particular circumstances.

As you will see, the development of early African-American musical traditions, vocal as well as instrumental, were influenced by the banjo. From the folk period that evolved before the mid-nineteenth century, to the early twentieth century and beyond, the banjo has been a player.

Second, the contemporary banjo is a true mixture of the interactions that took place between European and African communities. Joel Walker Sweeney and Dan Emmett, the two most prominent and influential white banjo players of the early nineteenth century, learned to play the banjo from African-Americans. Sweeney is credited with beginning the transformation of the banjo from an exclusively black instrument to one that is now synonymous with whites. As Elizabeth Baroody states, "Joel Sweeney was the first to recognize the musical genius of the Negro and his show, featuring those same slaves with whom he first made music, was accepted all over the South."[4]

Third, the method of playing the instrument lends itself to both an African and European style, the former being rhythm and the latter being melody and harmony.[5] It can be played as a solo instrument or as part of a larger group. Historically, the instrument was played during social occasions such as dances, parties, balls, and other gatherings. It was at these occasions that the formulation of a community identity was created, especially in the non-religious world. As African-American musical styles developed and matured, the banjo played a major role, especially in popularization of folk music, blues, ragtime, and jazz.[6]

Fourth, the banjo is important because it can be as individual as the person who plays it. It really began as a solo instrument. In early America, it provided a temporary escape from the stresses of slavery such as, broken families, violence, death, dismemberment, disease, and a denial of the basic freedoms we all now enjoy.

Early banjos were all home-made instruments. They were not mass-produced in a factory until the nineteenth century. Everything about the instrument—the way it was made, the way it was played, and the music that was made on it—spoke to individual expression because the banjo so readily lends itself to individual creativity. It also was an instrument that encouraged group song. The banjo was used at countless dances and gatherings of African-Americans who not only moved to the music but also sang along and responded to the lead of the musician. Indeed the griots of West Africa during the eighteenth and nineteenth centuries were the original "rappers." Their ability to improvise verse, music, and song in praise of tribal members or leaders is well documented. Because the African-American banjo playing tradition was not tied to formal musical notation and was improvisational, it could be adapted to the needs of whomever played it no matter what their level of education or sophistication. Truly a folk instrument, the banjo expressed the music of ordinary people in all its sentimentality, anger, alienation, joys, and dreams.

In fact, it could be argued that we have learned more from the lives of folk musicians than we have from professional performers. Their playing is more in keeping with their personal feelings and desires rather than their ability to please the expectations of an audience. This individual expression became very desirable in slave societies. These were places so oppressive that every thought, every move and action, was controlled by the slave owner or his representative. The banjo, and music in general, provided a respite from the deliberate oppression that was so commonplace in the enslavement of Africans and Americans. Like the spiritual in the religious world, the banjo provided temporary freedom in an African-American world that had very little of it.

In 1841 Solomon Northup, a free black man living in Saratoga, New York, was captured and enslaved in Louisiana for twelve years. During the years he was enslaved and trying to acquire his freedom, it was his instrument (in this case a fiddle) that gave him the strength (and considerable advantages) that he could find nowhere else.

Alas! Had it not been for my beloved violin, I scarcely can conceive how I could have endured the long years of bondage. It introduced me to great houses—relieved me of

many days' labor in the field—supplied me with conveniences for my cabin—with
pipes and tobacco, and extra pair of shoes, and oftentimes led me away from the presence
of a hard master, to witness scenes of jollity and mirth. It was my companion—the
friend of my bosom—triumphing loudly when I was joyful, and uttering its soft,
melodious consolations when I was sad. Often at midnight, when sleep had fled
affrighted from the cabin, and my soul was disturbed and troubled with the contem-
plation of my fate, it would sing me a song of peace. On Holy Sabbath days, when
an hour or two of leisure was allowed, it would accompany me to some quiet place on
the bayou bank, and, lifting up its voice, discourse kindly and pleasantly indeed.[7]

Throughout its history in America, the banjo and its music has represented a freedom of expression that was not available in many other ways, especially in early America. As a form of recreation within the slave community, it was second only to the fiddle as the instrument of choice.

As you will see, emancipation brought about another change in the black community. That shift and the overwhelming popularity of the minstrel stage changed the position of the banjo from an instrument of freedom to an instrument of slavery. The banjo has never regained its former status. It is that change in the perception of the banjo in the African-American community that caused it to lose favor. In the African-American struggle for acceptance and full citizenship after emancipation, the banjo was seen as an obstacle to overcome. Even its influence on the development of ragtime music, which Rupert Hughes call "banjo figurations," as well as its inclusion in the big band sound of the early twentieth century, did not give it the air of respectability that it deserved.[8]

Fifth, as African-Americans began to explore the world of work during the late nineteenth, and especially early twentieth century, the banjo was seen as a possible means of employment. As the promise of true freedom continued to elude African-Americans and they were forced to rely on a system of share-cropping, tenant farming, and other service-related jobs after emancipation, the possibility of the banjo as an alternative way of life was entertained by a few. As you will see, some were successful in their attempts to make a living with the banjo—many more were not.

Finally, the cultural background of the banjo should be studied to acknowledge its African beginnings. A growing number of historians now confirm that the banjo has its roots in the Senegambia region of West Africa. In a society in which history and fact continue to be contentious and questioned by every new author who has a point to prove (yours truly included), it is important to set the record straight. It is time that the banjo and its history are known to communities outside of practitioners and researchers. All Americans should understand and acknowledge the cultural heritage of African-Americans and the lasting influence they have had on the cultural landscape of the United States. The banjo is an integral part of that heritage.[9]

From slavery through emancipation, minstrelsy, segregation and civil rights, the banjo has been a part of the evolution of the African-American community. Developments that influenced its demise included the popularization of other musical instruments (chiefly the piano and guitar); new genres of musical expression such as ragtime, blues, jazz, and eventually popular music of all types (punk funk, rap, heavy metal, soul, hip hop, etc.); and, finally, the innovative and total acceptance of the instrument by the white Appalachian community.

All of these conditions combine to form the story of this book. That is what the deal is, and why it is so important to understand the banjo and its cultural evolution in the United States.

BY

HEWLETT & BRIGHT.

SALE OF

VALUABLE

SLAVES,

(On account of departure)

The Owner of the following named and valuable Slaves, being on the eve of departure for Europe, will cause the same to be offered for sale, at the NEW EXCHANGE, corner of St. Louis and Chartres streets, on *Saturday,* May 16, at Twelve o'Clock, *viz.*

1. SARAH, a mulatress, aged 45 years, a good cook and accustomed to house work in general, is an excellent and faithful nurse for sick persons, and in every respect a first rate character.

2. DENNIS, her son, a mulatto, aged 24 years, a first rate cook and steward for a vessel, having been in that capacity for many years on board one of the Mobile packets; is strictly honest, temperate, and a first rate subject.

3. CHOLE, a mulatress, aged 36 years, she is, without exception, one of the most competent servants in the country, a first rate washer and ironer, does up lace, a good cook, and for a bachelor who wishes a house-keeper she would be invaluable; she is also a good ladies' maid, having travelled to the North in that capacity.

4. FANNY, her daughter, a mulatress, aged 16 years, speaks French and English, is a superior hair-dresser, (pupil of Guillac,) a good seamstress and ladies' maid, is smart, intelligent, and a first rate character.

5. DANDRIDGE, a mulatoo, aged 26 years, a first rate dining-room servant, a good painter and rough carpenter, and has but few equals for honesty and sobriety.

6. NANCY, his wife, aged about 24 years, a confidential house servant, good seamstress, mantuamaker and tailoress, a good cook, washer and ironer, etc.

7. MARY ANN, her child, a creole, aged 7 years, speaks French and English, is smart, active and intelligent.

8. FANNY or FRANCES, a mulatress, aged 22 years, is a first rate washer and ironer, good cook and house servant, and has an excellent character.

9. EMMA, an orphan, aged 10 or 11 years, speaks French and English, has been in the country 7 years, has been accustomed to waiting on table, sewing etc.; is intelligent and active.

10. FRANK, a mulatto, aged about 32 years speaks French and English, is a first rate hostler and coachman, understands perfectly well the management of horses, and is, in every respect, a first rate character, with the exception that he will occasionally drink, though not an habitual drunkard.

All the above named Slaves are acclimated and excellent subjects; they were purchased by their present vendor many years ago, and will, therefore, be severally warranted against all vices and maladies prescribed by law, save and except FRANK, who is fully guaranteed in every other respect but the one above mentioned.

TERMS:—One-half Cash, and the other half in notes at six months, drawn and endorsed to the satisfaction of the Vendor, with special mortgage on the Slaves until final payment. The Acts of Sale to be passed before WILLIAM BOSWELL, Notary Public, at the expense of the Purchaser.

New-Orleans, May 13, 1835.

PRINTED BY BENJAMIN LEVY.

10

Although importation of slaves into the United States was made illegal in 1808, the buying and selling of slaves continued uninterrupted in the Southern states. Here, a notice offers slaves for sale in New Orleans, Louisiana, in 1835.

CHAPTER ONE

Black America and the Banjo Before 1900

Although African storytellers and musicians could be found in all areas of the continent of Africa, and called by many different names, the connections to the modern-day banjo has roots that are specific to the Senegambia region of West Africa. Historians link the banjo to West Africa and with people known as *griots*. This French word was commonly used to describe nomadic minstrels who lived in and around the Senegambia region of West Africa. These professional oral historians were experts in genealogy. They were also advisors to kings, confidants, praise-singers, and storytellers. "Gewel" is another term used in parts of Senegal that refers to musicians, entertainers, and storytellers. Many gewel and griots traveled from place to place and performed in the tradition of English troubadours, black bluesmen, folk musicians, and performers in early America.[10] Many were also prophets, soothsayers, and herbalists who used their talents to foretell the future as well as for healing.[11]

These African griots used an instrument called a *xalam* (pronounced halam) that historians now believe is the ancestor of the banjo. Enslaved Africans from the Wolof community, brought the knowledge of the xalam to the New World. That ethnic group provides the direct connection between the xalam and its descendant, the American banjo. The Wolof is the largest ethnic group in Senegal and its members were among the first Africans to be enslaved and brought to the New World.[12]

The xalam is a member of the lute family of instruments. It is a chordo-phone (which means its tone is created by the vibration of a string). The xalam is a small five-stringed instrument and is more oblong than round like the banjo. There are several types of lutes found in the Senegambian region. They include the molo, the guimbri, nkoni, gambare, and the kontingo.[13] The instruments are made from a single piece of carved wood. There is no separation between the body and the neck. The skin that forms the head of the body is usually calf or iguana. Both skins are very thin. The strings are traditionally calf's leather, but nylon strings are used today.

The xalam is the oldest stringed instrument in what is now the Senegambia region. Because so many instruments have migrated in and out of the country, there is some confusion about the regions many of the instruments originated in. The xalam is also older than the kora, a harp-like instrument with a large gourd body and wooden neck, which is the most popular instrument of the region today.[14]

As used in West Africa, the xalam was versatile, being used with both large and small groups. Performers could make up songs on the spot, adjust their playing to the tastes of their audience, intersperse the music with storytelling or dancing, or just play the instrument solo. The xalam was very percussive and rhythmic and lent itself to many types of call and response patterns (similar to counting cadence in the army where the leader begins a phrase and the audience, or soldiers in this case, repeat the phrase). Thus, the banjo is an instrument that comes out of a tradition of recreation, performance, and community interaction.

Ethnicity was the major way of distinguishing communities in Senegambia. Each group had its unique ways of expression. The clothes, language, and ways of interacting with each other differed. Many of these ethnic groups were brought to North America, mainly to Maryland, Virginia, South Carolina, North Carolina, and Georgia. These groups were very important to the early development of these areas of the American colonies. They included the Malinke, the Sereer, the Fulbe, the Soninke, the Bambara, and other speakers of the Mande language.[15] However, the Wolof represented most of the Senegambian slave trade, especially toward the end of the eighteenth century. During the 1730s, French and British slave traders shipped as many as two thousand Africans a year. The Wolof accounted for at least eighteen percent of that overall trade.[16]

Historian Dena Epstein mentions two English people who wrote from Sierra Leone in 1791. One was Nicholas Owens, a slave dealer in Africa from 1746 to 1757, and the other was Anna Maria Falconbridge. Both mention the banjo. They called it a *bangelo* and *bangeon,* and described it as "resembling our guitar."[17] Owens reported this fact between 1746–57 and Falconbridge in 1791.[18]

Initially, the banjo was taken to Caribbean countries such as Martinique, Jamaica, Haiti, Barbados, and finally to Maryland and Virginia. In colonial North America, the banjo seems to have had a regional focus that is particular to the Chesapeake Bay area of Virginia and Maryland. From roughly 1740 to 1840, the banjo, banjar, banjun, strum strum, and merrywang were used exclusively by enslaved Africans.

The earliest reference to the banjo in the New World (North America, South America, and the Caribbean) is found in the seventeenth century. Sir Hans Sloane mentions it in 1688 as existing in Barbados, Jamaica, and Martinique. It was referred to as a strum strum, banza, banjer, and banjar.[19] Even then it was used as an instrument of both individual and group expression.

From the very beginning of African-American enslavement, the music of black Americans was seen by their European captors as inferior. There was no acknowledgment of the significance of African-American music, other than relating it to the world of work, curiosity, or "scientific inquiry."

Colonial figures such as Nicholas Creswell, Thomas Jefferson, and Phillip Fithian did, however paternalistically, mention the banjo and its prominence as an instrument of the slaves. In his journal, Creswell wrote:

> *Mr. Bayley and I went to see a Negro Ball. Sundays being the only days these poor creatures have to themselves, they generally meet together and amuse themselves with Dancing to the Banjo. This musical instrument (if it may be so called) is made of a Gourd something in the imitation of a Guitar, with only four strings and played with the fingers in the same manner. Some of them sing to it, which is very droll music indeed. In their songs they generally relate the usage they have received from their masters and mistresses in a very satirical stile and manner. . . . They all appear to be exceedingly happy at these merry-makings and seem if they had forgot or were not sensible of their miserable condition.[20]*

Thomas Jefferson also mentioned the importance of the banjo to the African-American community and also acknowledged its African origins:

> *The instrument proper to them is the Banjar, which they brought hither from Africa, and which is the original of the guitar, its chords being precisely the four lower chords of the guitar.[21]*

Although the intermingling of the black and white culture did not happen immediately, it certainly did take place. The music of Europeans was heavily melodic and harmonic, not so of African music. African music, particularly music of West Africa, incorporated harmony and melody, but subordinated

Banjos were used to provide music at special occasions,
such as weddings. This watercolor painting shows the bride and groom about to
jump over a broomstick, which is part of the wedding ceremony.

them to rhythm. Within the white community, this basic tenet of black music was sharply discouraged and, in many instances, downright suppressed. However, the attempt was not successful because that rhythmic tradition manifested itself in literally every activity performed by blacks. From dancing and singing, for informal and formal gatherings, to the world of work, African-Americans permeated their lives with rhythm. Even religious songs learned from whites were given a rhythmic flavor peculiar to blacks.

In time, the cultures of the Irish, Scots, Germans, English, and other "new Americans" also experienced cross-fertilization. The result was Negro jigs (a type of colonial dance) such as "Pompey Ran Away," religious songs like "Lord I Want to Be a Christian," and others that could be "lined out."[22]

Blacks were even "hired out" (a colonial practice of leasing enslaved Africans and African-Americans to someone other than their owner, for a period of time) to provide the music for white balls and dances. Jigs, reels, quadrilles, waltzes, and the like were standard fare in black and white communities.

One of the first black music teachers during the colonial period was Newport Gardner (1746–1826). He was sold to Caleb Gardner, a successful white merchant from Newport, Rhode Island, at the age of fourteen and showed an aptitude for music. He was given music lessons at a young age and became proficient as a singer and composer. In 1791 he purchased his freedom and that of his family, rented a room, and opened a music school in Newport. Gardner became a deacon in the First Congregational Church and organized the Newport Colored Union Church and Society. In 1826 he traveled to Africa as a missionary and composed his most popular song, "Crooked Shanks."[23]

As early as 1654, the banjo (called banza) is mentioned in Barbados and Jamaica.[24] In 1774, the term "merrywang" is used by Edward Long, who wrote a history of Jamaica, for an instrument he said was a "rustic guitar of four strings . . . made with a calibash . . . a hand . . . with a sort of rude carved work, and ribbands."[25] In 1784 Johann Schoepf mentions an instrument called a banjah in the Bahamas. Luffman mentions the banjah in Antigua.[26]

On the islands of St. Vincent, St. Thomas, Guiana, and Jamaica, and in British Guiana, Christmas celebrations among African-Americans included music and dancing with banjo-like instruments:

> . . . they again assembled on the lawn before the house with their gombays, bonjaws, and an ebo drum. . . . Some of the women carried small calabashes with pebbles in them, stuck on short sticks, which they rattled in time to the songs. . . .[27]

Jamaica, the island where the banjo was most common, was also known for its celebration of "John Canoe." This was part of the Christmas celebration and was thought to originate from Africa:

In the towns, during Christmas holidays, they have several tall robust fellows dressed up in grotesque habits, and a pair of ox-horns on their head, sprouting from the top of a horrid sort of vizor, or mask, which about the mouth is rendered very terrific with large boar-tusk. . . . He dances at every door, bellowing out John Connu! With great vehemence. . . . [28]

The expectation was that some gift or reward would be given to African-Americans in celebration of the holiday season.

In 1774, Nicholas Creswell also described the same kind of instrument seen in Jamaica, in Maryland, but it was referred to as a banjo.[29] Reverend Jonathan Boucher, a British philologist, began a supplement to a dictionary by Dr. Johnson that was never finished, but he did get to the b's and defined *bandore* as,

A musical instrument . . . in use chiefly, if not entirely, among people of the lower classes. . . . I well remember, that in Virginia and Maryland the favourite and almost only instrument in use among the slaves there was a bandore; or, as they pronounced the word, banjer. Its body was a large hollow gourd, with a long handle attached to it strung with catgut, and played on with the fingers. . . . My memory supplies me with a couplet of one of their songs, which are generally of the improvisatori kind; nor did I use to think the poetry much beneath the music:

Negro Sambo play fine banjer,
Make his fingers go like handsaw.[30]

Life for enslaved blacks during the colonial period was oppressive. Ripped from their homes, brought in chains to the shores of the Caribbean, South and North America, their lot, while better in North America than in many other

New World colonies, was still dreadful. Whether life was filled with work that harvested tobacco, rice, indigo, sugar cane, or domestic crops like corn, wheat, or cotton, it was severe. As John F. D. Smyth described in 1784 in *A Tour in the United States of America*:

> *The Negro is called up about daybreak, and is seldom allowed time enough to swallow three mouthfuls of homminy, or hoe-cake, but is driven out immediately to the field of hard labor . . . the noon meal . . . [consists of] homminy and salt and, if his master be a man of humanity, he has a little fat, skimmed milk, rusty bacon or salt herring to relish his homminy or hoecake. . . . They then return to severe labour . . . until dusk in the evening, when they repair to the tobacco-houses, where each has his task in stripping allotted him, which employs him some hours. . . . It is late at night before he returns to his second scanty meal.*[31]

Such was the life that most African-Americans lived during the colonial period. But how did they survive? How did music, and particularly the banjo, aid them in acquiring moments of freedom in the midst of slavery? How did music support them during the work day and how did it help them find solace in the dark of night when there was nothing but the groans of aching bones and tired muscles to lull them to sleep? These are the questions that have led me to investigate the role of the banjo in the experience of African-Americans.

In the eighteenth century, according to Winans, 709 black musicians were mentioned in runaway slave ads. Of those he found only seventeen banjo players and eleven of them were from the Chesapeake Bay area.[32]

From the 1740s to the beginning of the twentieth century, African-Americans were seen as the primary players of the banjo. According to Lawrence Levine, African-American music achieved its highest artistic level musically, with song, particularly the spiritual. Perhaps that is because it was seen as a form that was not sung, adapted, or used primarily for the benefit of an audience. The spiritual was highly personal and deeply religious in its creation and delivery. They were

PICKING.

Slaves worked from sunrise to sunset in blistering heat.
This drawing shows an overseer on horseback following field slaves.

for those who had given up a secular life and dedicated their lives to God.[33] Instrumental folk music in popular culture was tainted because of its association with social dance and secular pursuits. The folksong, as one source termed it, "was considered the wildflower of the musical art—ennobled by its natural simplicity." [34]

So the banjo as an instrument of the black community was not considered a part of any serious or scholarly discussion of music in a manner that paralleled African-American vocal and religious music. It was seen as a folk instrument, and those who played it were considered roustabouts, itinerants, and merely entertainers. Unfortunately, this perception set the stage for "interpretations" of African-American people that were degrading, stereotypical, and mean-spirited. As the world of entertainment became more sophisticated and more and more performers saw it as a way to make a living, African-Americans, and particularly former slaves, would figure prominently in a new form of entertainment called minstrelsy. Not only would minstrel performers taint popular perceptions of African-Americans, they would also use as their primary tool of musical expression, the banjo. It was the banjo's connection to minstrel performances all over the world that would make it the bane of progressive-minded African-Americans across the nation.

The Nineteenth Century

By the beginning of the nineteenth century, the population of the United States had reached about 4 million. Of that number, about 893,602 were of African ancestry. The majority of that number (almost ninety percent), lived in the South Atlantic states. Virginia and South Carolina had the largest number.

Because of soil depletion and a market glutted with products, the price of slaves had declined and there was widespread belief that the institution of slavery would end as a result. Many scholars believe it was the invention and development of the cotton gin, by a Northern school teacher named Eli Whitney, that would change an economic system that had depended on other "cash crops" to sustain the economy. As a result of the cotton gin (which made cotton production more economical), and the corresponding spread of cotton growing, the need for slave labor to service it also increased. Although the importation of slaves into the United States ended January 1, 1808, the domestic trade actually increased.[35]

African-American music was undergoing changes as well. After the American Revolution and especially the War of 1812, concerts, plays, and operas had

Music from a banjo sometimes helped slaves get through the day.
This drawing, made in the 1860s, shows slaves gathering around another worker
who is singing and playing the banjo.

begun to flourish. In the black community the emergence of black churches, black denominations, black hymnbooks, and activities such as camp meetings had begun to influence the creation of black musical styles and methods of worship. But something was also happening in the secular world of American culture in general.

A New America

After the war of 1812, Americans began searching for a culture that was unique to them. They sought a common experience that glorified white American democracy. This was a culture not tied to the elite, learned, and aristocratic society that had so completely dominated the Colonial period. It was a culture that glorified the "lowbrow" instead of the "highbrow."

Lowbrow culture found its believers in those who thought that after the Revolution, America had emerged as a strong democratic nation that was unique and different from its European progenitors. This group of Americans wanted to create a culture that was not based on European standards with its aristocratic gentlemen and the way they turned up their noses at people who were not as refined as they felt themselves to be. A new economic stability in America had convinced this group that they would not have to depend on Britain, France, Spain, or any other powers to maintain national stability. With this new economic independence came a desire to identify Americans as a unique nation made up of people, goods, information, and ideas that did not seek an identity based on outside models but grounded in a new American image that glorified the common man—the common white man.

For those who catered to the standards of highbrow society, they saw America as aspiring to the highest standards possible. This was a community of rich, aristocratic elites who made up a small percentage of the population but wielded a considerable amount of clout. They were the businessmen, the politicians, the industrialists, the moneymakers, and the lawgivers. It was their clout and their support that was needed to create and maintain America's new interest in the "average" American. They owned the newspapers, the factories, the railroads, the shipping lines, the publications, and the theaters that would model, legislate, and champion the behaviors of a new Everyman.

Between 1820–1840, cities like Philadelphia, New York, Boston, and Washington, D.C. experienced phenomenal growth. These new urban (and initially white) dwellers had sought to redefine their culture. In places like New York, these "original" Americans had begun to see a major influx of foreign-born people entering America. This emerging melting pot was jarring their sense of nationhood and increasing their desire to see themselves as Americans. The social and economic realities these new urban dwellers had grown accustomed to in the South had begun to change drastically. Alien environments, poor housing conditions, diseases, and low paying jobs, hastened the need for something that would unite them as unique, special, and privileged while holding on to ideas that represented them as common men. Gone were the jokes, stories, and songs they were used to. Gone were the values, beliefs, and rules they had lived by, as well as the labor force that had sustained their way of life. Gone was the affirmation that, even as an underprivileged class of white people, they were still privileged because they were white and American. What was left to do was to shape the country in their own image.

Nationalism, politics, social status, westward expansion, and economic and technical growth had begun to change American culture in significant ways and most of that change took place in the North. Technical growth was realized through advances in the publishing industry as well as popular entertainment, which brought mass audiences into tents, lyceums, concert halls, and theaters, and particularly in America's urban centers. These representatives of the cultural media and an emerging popular culture tried to satisfy both classes of people, the ordinary American and the aristocrat, with articles, stories, prose, and presentations that glorified the common man. They also sought to affirm the dignity of the upper class, which in most cases sponsored, owned, or bankrolled the organizations themselves. But it would be the minstrel stage that would take the concept of American entertainment and the democratic ideal to another level.

Public Sale.

BY order of the Orphans' Court of Anne Arundel County, the subscriber will expose at Public Sale, on Tuesday, the 4th of October next, all the personal property of Joshua Howard, late of said county, deceased, consisting of

TWELVE NEGROES,

CONSISTING OF

Men, Women, and Children, *HORSES, CATTLE, SHEEP, &*

HOGS,
One Wagon

AND
GEARS,
One Yoke of Oxen
AND
CART

with a variety of FARMING UTENSILS HOUSEHOLD AND KITCHEN FURNITURE, Wheat, Rye, and Oats in the Straw; a crop of Tobacco, and a crop of Corn, also a great many other articles too tedious to mention.

Terms of Sale.

All sums of twenty dollars and upwards, six months credit, the purchasers giving note with approved security. All sums under twenty dollars cash.
MARY HOWARD,
Executrix,
September 21.

As this notice shows, slaves were often sold at public auction, along with other kinds of property, such as livestock and wagons.

The Minstrel Phenomenon

In the nineteenth century, many people acknowledged the genius of the African-American musical tradition. The antebellum years did not diminish the importance of black musical expression, especially their songs, which were referred to as, "Ethiopian melodies." In 1845, J. Kinnard wrote in *Knickerbocker Magazine:*

> *Who are our true rulers? The Negro poets, to be sure. Do they not set the fashion, and give laws to the public taste? Let one of them, in the swamps of Carolina, compose a new song, and it no sooner reaches the ear of a white amateur, than it is written down, amended (that is, almost spoilt), printed, and then put upon a course of rapid dissemination, to cease only with the utmost bounds of Anglo-Saxondom, perhaps with the world. Meanwhile, the poor author digs away with his hoe, utterly ignorant of his greatness.*[36]

However, Kinnard's sentiments, while acknowledging the literary talents of African-Americans, did very little to improve the living conditions of enslaved African-Americans. They were still slaves and still victimized by their owners. Ironically, even though the slave trade ended in 1808, a domestic and transatlantic slave trade still flourished many years after that date, especially in places like South Carolina.[37]

The term "Jim Crow" became a way white Southerners used to keep blacks in a position of polit-

*This photo was taken during the Civil War. These slaves are
planting sweet potatoes on a plantation in South Carolina. Some of the slaves
wore parts of uniforms taken from Union soldiers.*

ical, economic, and social subservience. Jim Crow began as an imitation of a
black man who lived in Kentucky. The character was subsequently developed
for the minstrel stage. In time, however, Jim Crow became a symbol that was
synonymous with racial oppression and a desire to deny African-Americans full
citizenship.

Jim Crow was popularized by an actor named Thomas Dartmouth Rice. In
1831, he observed an African-American dancing on the Cincinnati levee.[38] As
he danced, he sang a little song:

Wheel about turn about;
Do just so;
An' ebery time I turn about
I dance Jim Crow.[39]

This African-American man worked in a stable in Louisville, Kentucky, and he unwittingly began the phenomenon known as Jim Crow. The stable was adjacent to the Louisville Theatre where performers presented shows. Rice, who is credited with popularizing minstrel performances, was there for a show. He was a professional actor. He recalled what he witnessed and how Jim's antics affected him:

> *The actors could look into the stable yard from the windows of their dressing rooms and were fond of watching the movements of an old and decrepit slave who was employed by the proprietor to do odd jobs. The slave, who called himself Jim Crow, was physically deformed—the right shoulder was drawn up high, and the left leg was stiff and crooked at the knee. As he walked with his painful, but at the same time ludicrous, limp, he was in the habit of crooning an old tune, to which he had applied words of his own. At the end of each verse he gave a peculiar step, "rocking de heel" in the manner that has since become so general among the long generation of his delineators.*[40]

Upon seeing this, Rice decided to include a version of this character in his own stage act. His portrayal of a black buffoon was so popular among white audiences that it became the term used to refer to Southern whites' attempts to keep blacks "in their place." Rice, who was a struggling performer before that time, became one of the most celebrated entertainers of his day. His character was so popular that he was invited to perform in Great Britain. Jim Crow not only ushered in a new form of entertainment, it also became the term most frequently used during that period to represent segregation, especially relating to travel on Southern railroads.

Segregation took many forms. Southerners enacted laws against inter-marriage of the races throughout the South. Blacks and whites were separated on trains, in depots, and on wharves. With Federal troops leaving the South and a new spirit of conciliation brought about by a newly elected Democratic leadership, Congress removed many of the restrictions meant to protect the rights of African-Americans. In 1878, the use of armed forces during elections was removed. In 1894, Federal Marshals and special field supervisors who were put in place to regulate elections were discontinued. Four years later, all Southerners disloyal and rebellious to the Union were given amnesty.

Democrats used their new-found power to minimize the political power of African-Americans. The Fourteenth and Fifteenth Amendments to the Constitution made it difficult to legally refuse blacks the right to vote, so Democrats used other methods—some of which were outside the law and others that used powers that were established by individual states. For instance, Virginia, re-aligned, or gerrymandered, its voting districts five times in order to weaken the impact of the African-American vote. Poll taxes (taxes that had to be paid in order to be allowed to vote) and literacy tests—election procedures that required complex testing of blacks wishing to vote—were also enacted. In South Carolina, a complex series of voting boxes on ballots made it nearly impossible for semi-literate and illiterate voters to find the right box. No one was allowed to speak to a voter, and if he failed to find the correct box, his vote was thrown out.

For many white Southerners, violence was the best way to keep blacks from exercising their political rights. In countless communities, African-Americans were punished for even showing their faces near a voting area. H.W. Lewis of Mississippi wrote a letter to Governor Adelbert Ames explaining the situation in Columbia:

Dear Sir: Everything in this and adjoining counties is up to fever heat. The 24-pound cannon thunders forth every night. The brass band accompanies the democratic speakers, together with about 50 hot-headed young men, and assassination and blood-shed are openly encouraged. Our voters are very much overawed, and [we] fear we cannot get out more than one-half of them. If troops could be sent here, even a "corporal's guard," it would act like magic, and we would sweep everything in this part of the State. As it is, it looks as though we should lose everything. . . . If anything can be done, I know you will do it. If not, we shall do the best we can and try to meet the issue bravely.[41]

Mississippi, the state that had a black majority population, did many things to keep the power of the ballot away from African-Americans. In 1890, the state added a suffrage amendment to its state constitution. The amendment

imposed a poll tax of two dollars; excluded voters convicted of bribery, burglary, theft, arson, perjury, murder, or bigamy; and also barred all who could not read any section of the state constitution, or understand it when read, or give a reasonable interpretation of it.[42]

In 1883, African-Americans were not allowed in white hotels, barber shops, theaters, restaurants, stores, and other public buildings frequented by whites. As new state constitutions were set in place, African-Americans were effectively and completely segregated from whites.

What kind of entertainment could be so popular that it became an accepted and legitimate representation of American values? How could minstrelsy be so instrumental in fashioning and nurturing a social, political, and economic movement that defined popular culture for three-quarters of a century?

The minstrel show was extremely popular for several reasons: (1) It glorified folk culture; (2) It was highly responsive to the audience and encouraged audience participation; (3) It contained no plot, musical score, memorized speeches, or fixed script; (4) Each act was a skit, a joke, a song, or a dance; (5) It satisfied Northern whites' curiosity about blacks and slavery; (6) It was immediate,

In the 1840s, the Ethiopian Serenaders were white minstrels
in blackface makeup. One newspaper described the group: "They are painted jet black,
with ruddy lips, and large mouths . . . wagers have been offered that they are really 'darkies.'"
The newspaper identifies the banjo as an "African guitar."

unpretentious, and direct; (7) The material used was wild, energetic, and earthy; (8) It nurtured the white notion that no matter how pitiful their lot, they could take comfort in the fact that they were vastly different from, and superior to, blacks.[43]

Four other men, along with Rice, are generally credited with beginning blackface minstrelsy. It received that name because performers who portrayed African-Americans put burnt cork on their faces. They then put on costumes that included rags, gaudy colors, baggy shirts, and pants, and clown-like hats and gloves to duplicate the appearance of a slave character.

Joel Sweeney, Daniel Decatur Emmett, E.P. Christy, and William Whitlock are acknowledged as the first minstrel performers. Although he was not known as a minstrel performer, Stephen Foster deserves mention. Foster is important because he was a prolific songwriter. His songs were used extensively in most minstrel shows.

Ironically, minstrelsy, is the only dramatic art (if one can attach such a term to it) that has its origins in America.[44] According to William "Billy" Whitlock in his autobiography, the first minstrel performance took place in New York. His account goes this way:

> The organization of the minstrels I claim to be my own idea, and it cannot be blotted out. One day I asked Dan Emmett, who was in New York at the time, to practise the fiddle and the banjo with me at his boarding house in Catherine Street. We went down there, and, when we had practised, Frank Brower called in by accident. He listened to our music, charmed to his soul. I told him to join with the bones which he did. Presently Dick Pelham came in, also by accident, and looked amazed. I asked him to procure a tambourine and make one of the party, and he went out and got one. After practising for a while we went to the old resort of the circus crowd—the "Branch," in the Bowery and in Bartlett's billiard-room—with our instruments and performed for the first time as the Virginia Minstrels. A programme was made out, at the first time

we appeared upon the stage before an audience was for the benefit of Pelham at the Chatham Theatre. The house was crammed—jammed with our friends; and Dick, of course, put ducats in his purse. According to Dan Emmett, this was the Spring of 1843.[45]

The popularity of minstrelsy was a result of the conventions it used as well as the satirical social and political themes it forwarded. As Alexander Saxton asserts:

Taken as a whole, the genre provided a kind of underground theater where the blackface [sic] "convention" rendered permissible topics which would have been taboo on the legitimate stage or in the press. Spontaneity and ad-libbing favored a flexible approach in different audiences and regions, changing moods and times. This combination of adaptiveness and liberty of subject matter explains in part the popularity and staying power of minstrelsy as mass entertainment.[46]

The Politics of Blackface

It is no accident that minstrelsy was used to forward the political ideals of the Democratic Party. The Whig, Liberty, Free-Soil, Native American, and Republican parties had always opposed the Democratic Party. The Democratic Party, in turn, did not support notions of temperance. Instead, Democrats supported European immigration and territorial expansion. This ideology was what the Jacksonian philosophy was built on and minstrelsy supported that doctrine.

Before the Civil War, the Democratic Party was the most popular political party. It had control of the Federal government and did all it could to keep it. The key to control was maintaining party unity among regional branches of the Federal government. The Democratic Party, which had been in existence since the late eighteenth century, supported the strict enforcement of Constitutional laws. The policies of the Democratic Party could not succeed unless all of the states it represented believed in those policies. Their goal, from the beginning, was to establish a party system that would be representative of the North as well as of the South. If the party was to succeed it needed to create policies that all Democrats, regardless of where they lived, could support.

If Southern Democrats were to support the party, they demanded that the national party defend the institution of slavery.[47] And we must not forget that it was the "walk around" song "Dixie" (that traditionally is accepted as being authored in 1859 by Dan Emmett) that coincidentally was introduced on the eve of the Civil War and became the national anthem of the Confederacy.[48]

Since most minstrels were Northerners, as were most of their audiences, the Democrats also sought to sabotage the work of the abolitionists. Northern leaders wanted to resist criticisms of slavery and prevent antislavery proponents from being successful in their recruitment efforts. Abolitionists themselves, especially during the Civil War, were portrayed on the minstrel stage as ignorant, hypocritical, loyalists, and supporters of miscegenation.[49]

With these beliefs clearly ensconced, it is no wonder that the minstrel show was built on a loosely contrived plot that introduced "darkies" who loved their masters; longed to return to the plantation when "forced" to leave; dreaded freedom; could not think for themselves and were naturally docile and feeble-minded. The whole idea was to make Northern audiences believe that freedom and upward mobility for blacks was as ridiculous as they themselves were.[50]

In short, the South was the appropriate home of blacks, and this home was devoid of any culture or history of that community. African-Americans were seen as a part of the landscape of the Old South, a place of simplicity, happiness, childlike comfort, and joy:

> *Down by the river our log hut stands*
> *Where father and mother once dwelt*

One of the most popular blackface minstrel groups was George Thatcher's Greatest Minstrels. This poster displays the exaggerated portrayal of African-Americans that white audiences expected.

And the old door latch that was worn by our hands
And the church where in prayer we knelt. [51]

Some antislavery sentiment did exist in minstrelsy, especially in early songs that were more directly borrowed from the black community rather than written outside of it. Such sentiment was evident in songs such as "The Raccoon Hunt."

My ole massa dead and gone,
A dose of poison help him on
De debil say he funeral song. [52]

A second way minstrelsy advanced antislavery notions was through themes that dealt seriously with love, intimacy, and separation of families through the prism of sentimentality. But even these songs seldom made mention of slavery in particular.

The Sweeney Boys

Joel Walker Sweeney is considered by many to be the father of the modern banjo and the father of American minstrelsy. Sweeney was born in Buckingham County, Virginia, in 1813, not far from the Appomattox Court House. By the time he was thirteen, he could play on the four-string gourd banjo, an instrument used exclusively by colonial blacks. He had two brothers, Sam and Richard, and they played as well. Neither of his parents played music but Sweeney, having grown up around enslaved Africans, learned their music and eventually adapted their instrument.

Around 1831 Sweeney made a banjo of wood and added a base string. In the beginning he attended the county courts in Buckingham that maintained the eighteenth-century tradition of having all types of entertainment during those occasions when the county courts met. These "Court Days" provided the perfect opportunity for Sweeney to try the music and style he adopted from his black mentors.

By 1840 Sweeney had entered the professional ranks. He joined a small circus and traveled through Virginia and North Carolina singing and playing. Eventually he moved north and finally toured England. His troupe, called "Old Joe's Company," joined the extremely popular minstrel circuit and performed into the 1890s. Judge R.B. Pore of Appomattox Court House, remembered Sweeney and said of him:

> *Joe Sweeney was a fine delineator of the Negro character. Raised as he was in the midst of them and possessing a quick observation and a keen sense of the ludicrous, he made his concerts very attractive, because his manners and language were so true to the original. Nearly all the leading minstrels who have since met with success, at one time or another belonged to Old Joe's Band.* [53]

Like early black banjo players, Sweeney played the instrument without the benefit of notes or written music. Fred Mather, who was a contemporary of Sweeney and also a minstrel and banjoist, wrote in 1897:

> *I do not read music but can spell it out painfully, not by note. In the long ago, when I was a fair manipulator of the "gourd shell," I remember only three banjoists who read notes. They were Dan Emmett, G. Swayne Buckely and Frank B. Converse, who, by the way, was on the stage but a short time. Joe Sweeney didn't know a note, nor did most of the banjoists of 40 or 50 years ago. In fact, when I was a boy, I often heard it said: "There are no notes to a banjo, you just play it."* [54]

Sweeney's brother Sam enjoyed considerable notoriety playing the banjo himself, especially during the Civil War. Joel died before the war began. He is buried at Appomattox Court House.[55]

Young Sam fought for the Southern cause in the Virginia Cavalry. His skill with the banjo captivated General J.E.B. Stuart.[56] Stuart, who enjoyed a good show and loved to be entertained, especially with music, couldn't get enough of Sam's banjo playing. W.W. Blackford, who was an officer under Stuart's command, remembered Stuart's love of entertainment and his soft spot for Sam Sweeney:

> *He collected around him a number of experts, not only in music but theatricals and tricks of various kinds, and they added much to the pleasure of camp life. Sweeney and his banjo and his Negro melodies were the favorites; and Sweeney always carried his instrument slung at his back on marches, and often in long night marches, the life of the men was restored by its tinkle.*[57]

Stephen Vincent Benét even mentions Sam in his epic poem, "John Brown's Body."[58] Sweeney played for Stuart until his death and then continued to play for his fellow soldiers until he died of smallpox in 1860.

The Minstrel Stage, African-Americans, and the Civil War

By contrast the minstrel stage did all it could to portray African-Americans as cowards who, if allowed to fight, would surely flee at the first sign of serious firepower.

> *Niggers dey can pick cotton—dey'll do it very freely*
> *But when dey smell de bullets, how dey'll run for Horace Greely!*[59]

The 54th Massachusetts Regiment and other all-black units would prove this perception to be wrong. It was their bravery that convinced white Northerners, especially their fellow white soldiers, that they were not only willing to fight but could hold their own in the face of extremely overwhelming odds.

It was on the evening of July 18, 1863, that the 54th proved its bravery, determination, and love of country. This was the first African-American regiment to attack a virtually impenetrable fortress near Charleston, South Carolina, called Fort Wagner. They began the battle at nightfall that hot evening of July eighteenth. Six hours later, at 2 A.M. the next morning, they were ordered to retreat. For six hours, they fought and died. At the end of the battle the Confederates had lost one hundred and eighty-one soldiers, the 54th had lost 1,515. Twenty-two year old Sgt. William Carney bore the flag from the top of the parapet and carried it until the order was given to retreat. With the American flag battered, torn, and faded, the wounded Carney limped back to the Union camp on the other side of the parapet. The only words he spoke once he arrived at the camp were "Boys, the old flag never touched the ground." For his bravery, Sgt. Carney of company C, 54th Massachusetts, was given the Medal of Honor. He was the first African-American in the history of the United States to receive this honor. With nothing but a flag and an indomitable spirit, he won the army's highest commendation.[60]

Groups such as the 54th Massachusetts, the 101st Arkansas, the 1st South Carolina Volunteers, the 65th Colored Infantry, the 5th United States Colored Heavy Artillery, and many others (soldiers and sailors) showed their mettle during the Civil War. In the end, 38,000 black soldiers lost their lives in the Civil War and their rate of mortality was nearly forty percent greater than that of white soldiers, but you would not have known that fact if you received your information from the minstrel stage. During the war, on the minstrel stage, African-Americans were portrayed as pickpockets, crooked politicians, carpetbaggers, draft dodgers, and deserters.

This oppression and racial discrimination, although primarily aimed at blacks, also extended to Native Americans, Asians, and Mexicans during the period of, and immediately following, the Civil War. Blackface minstrelsy was more than seventy years of puppetry with white supremacists acting as the puppet masters.

In 1896, the Supreme Court added another nail to the coffin of inequity in its decision regarding *Plessy versus Ferguson.* In this case, Homer Adolph Plessy was arrested in the state of Louisiana for refusing to ride in the "Jim Crow" (colored only) section of a passenger train. His refusal was a violation of the Louisiana law requiring segregated seating for blacks. The Court decided that separate facilities were not unlawful, or a violation of the Fourteenth Amendment, as long as facilities provided for blacks were equal to those of whites.

The Supreme Court's ruling was followed by an anxious public, and for many white Americans, the majority decision of the judges sitting on the bench was a relief. Justice Henry B. Brown spoke for them:

> *We consider the underlying fallacy of the plaintiff's argument to consist in the assumption that the enforced separation of the two races stamps the colored race with a badge of inferiority. If this be so, it is not by reason of anything found in the act, but solely because the colored race chooses to put that construction upon it.* [61]

He did not speak for all of the justices however. In a dissenting opinion, Justice John M. Harlan felt the underlying motivation had less to do with the perceptions of African-Americans and more to do with racial attitudes of the day:

> *What can more certainly arouse race hate, what more certainly create and perpetuate a feeling of distrust between these races, than state enactments, which, in fact, proceed on the ground that colored citizens are so inferior and degraded that they cannot be allowed to sit in public coaches occupied by white citizens? That, as all will admit, is the real meaning of such legislation as was enacted in Louisiana.* [62]

Such was the atmosphere that fueled the enormous popularity of the minstrel stage. If minstrel performers needed any evidence that they were on the right track in their pursuit of popular notions of race in America, they needed it no longer.

Stephen Foster and *Uncle Tom's Cabin*

One of the few images that contradicted the nineteenth-century image of African-Americans as the gambling, watermelon-eating, fighting, razor-toting, chicken-stealing, grinning buffoons who sang coon songs such as "Hello, My Baby," was Stephen Foster and *Uncle Tom's Cabin* by Harriet Beecher Stowe. Foster was the most popular white minstrel composer of his time. Called "America's Troubadour," he began writing at an early age. Foster came into contact with the music of African-Americans as a child. The family servant, Olivia Pise, regularly took him to African-American church services. As a songwriter, he based many of the songs he composed on tunes that were popular in the black community. Many of his songs, including "Old Black Joe," "Camptown Races," "My Old Kentucky Home," "Old Folks at Home," and "Massa's in the Cold Cold Ground," were inspired by those associations.[63]

Both Foster and *Uncle Tom's Cabin* suggested a view of the Southern black that was sentimental and bordering on the heroic. These romantic racial stereotypes were certainly not what Frederick Douglass, James Weldon Johnson, W.E.B. Du Bois, and others were hoping for as representations of the "Talented Tenth," but they were welcome images when compared to the emasculation perpetuated by the minstrel stage.[64] The legacy of the Uncle Tom character that survives to this day is certainly a negative image, but in the 1890s it was a welcome change from the status quo. Songs such as "My Old Kentucky Home," "Old Folks at Home," and "Old Black Joe" had long associations with the famous play. The fact that it played for seventy-seven years attests to the phenomenal impact it had in America and abroad. From 1852 to 1931 it captured the imagination of the world.[65]

Uncle Tom's Cabin not only glorified the South as something other than an oppressor and usurper of slavery, it redeemed the Southern white slave owner and the black slave as people caught up in a complex, dehumanized climate that many were trying their best to deal with. It was neither black nor white, but shades of gray. It was a morality play, a vehicle for social reform, and it had entertaining, unforgettable characters. There was something for everyone. Slave owners and slaves were portrayed as three-dimensional characters in Stowe's novel. They became cultural archetypes and pushed the American literary community to new levels of expression and helped redefine the South in the eyes of the world. Although the banjo is not mentioned in *Uncle Tom's Cabin,* it was a consistent element in every production, so strongly was it seen as an instrument of the plantation black.[66]

Music was the one attribute white Americans readily admitted African-Americans excelled in. As early as 1856, the musical genius of African-Americans was acknowledged:

> The only musical population of the country are the negroes of the South. Here at the North we have teachers in great numbers, who try to graft the love of music upon the tastes of our colder race . . . the Negro is a natural musician. . . . The African nature is full of poetry. Inferior to the white race in reason and manner. In this they resemble the southern nations of Europe. . . . Might not our countrymen all learn a lesson from these simple children of Africa? We are a silent and reserved people. . . . Songless and joyless, the [white] laborer goes to his task.[67]

Meanwhile newly freed blacks struggled with their own identity and their relationship with the banjo.

The transition from slavery to freedom was a difficult one for African-American men. It was a time of adjustment from what was to the hope of what could be. African-Americans struggled to improve their economic condition, but the major struggle was gaining the respect of a hostile white society convinced of their inferiority. Black writers and white sympathizers endeavored to point out the accomplishments of African-Americans who had distinguished themselves, as proof that the potential to rise above the chains of slavery was not only possible but inevitable. They tried to convince a skeptical majority that color was not connected to aptitude. They pointed out Benjamin Banneker (1731–1806), the mathematician and astronomer; James Derham (1762–?), the first black physician in the nation; Reverend Prince Hall (1735–1807), founder of Negro freemasonry; to the poets Phillis Wheatley (1753–1794) and Jupiter Hammon (1717–1787); and the writer Olaudah Equiano (Gustavus Vassa, 1745–1801). But these examples too often were not enough to sway the entrenched thinking of former slave owners and others who connected blacks to slavery, Africa, and barbarism.

African-American Reaction to the Minstrel Stage

In stark contrast to the minstrel notion of blacks, particularly in the city of New York where it flourished, was the maiming and lynching of blacks on the sidewalks of New York during the draft riots of 1863.[68] In July of that year, three thousand longshoremen went on strike for higher pay. African-Americans were hired to take their place, with the protection of the police. Because the Civil War was already in progress, the unemployed longshoremen were drafted into the Union army. The insult of having their jobs taken by African-Americans and then having to go to battle and risk their lives for black emancipation was too much to bear and a riot broke out. The riot lasted four days, from July thirteenth to the sixteenth, before authorities were able to bring it under control. African-American homes and businesses were burned and over one thousand people died.[69]

In the nineteenth century, black music had matured to a degree that it was being seen as novel. The African-American musical experience evolved from an oral tradition that stretched back to Africa, so much of the thoughts, expressions, hopes, desires, and teaching were transmitted orally. If anyone wanted to understand African-American culture, it was important to listen to their music.

Their singing was not simply the result of a need to entertain, it was a result of a need to express concerns, challenges, and hopes and fears that were best expressed in the form of music. W.E.B. Du Bois' comment that music was the slave's message to the world was appropriately stated, for in their musical expression was the multiplicity of thoughts that could not be expressed in written form as skillfully as it could in oral form.

> *I know little of music and can say nothing in technical phrase, but I know something of men, and knowing them, I know that these songs are the articulate message of the slave to the world. They tell us in these days that life was joyous to the black slave, careless and happy. I can easily believe this of some, of many. But not all the past South, though it rose from the dead, could gainsay the heart-touching witness of these songs. They are the music of an unhappy people, of the children of disappointment; they tell of death and suffering, and unvoiced longing toward a truer world, of misty wanderings and hidden ways.*[70]

This importance of song was also carried forward in African-American banjo playing of the nineteenth century. Before the minstrel stage, most music from the European tradition was divided. Either one sang or played an instrument. African-Americans began using music as an accompaniment to singing, and the words became as important an element as the music.[71] Together, they expressed feelings and perceptions that neither could do effectively alone. This style was taken by white minstrel performers and used as a method of entertaining rather than as a desire to communicate the longings of an oppressed community of people. Thus, much of the black musical experience of the nineteenth century is eclipsed by the phenomenal popularity of the minstrel stage.

However, it also must be reiterated that although minstrelsy had its beginnings in trying to imitate the "plantation Negro," it was more successful at caricaturing the urban free black. It then spun off into various directions that

*Some minstrel shows were lavish productions, complete with scenery
and large casts. These large shows were usually based on a farcical portrayal of backwoods
life on a Southern plantation. This show included white cast members, plus
white actors in blackface wearing straw hats and overalls.*

created a new genre of performance rather than being faithful to cultural norms within the African-American community.

For most of the period of its popularity (1850–1920), minstrelsy was a slave to popular culture and mass consumption that related to the "democratic ideal." Around 1855, black men began to take the minstrel stage. They became extremely popular around 1880. Because Northern whites were curious about newly freed blacks, they flocked to shows that featured them. Because blacks had been portrayed by white men on the minstrel stage, the opportunity to see "authentic" blacks portraying themselves became enticing, not only to blacks

This photo shows two blackface minstrels impersonating African-Americans. Minstrels often portrayed African-Americans wearing ragged costumes and having downcast expressions.

who wanted to perform but to promoters who were looking for an angle to outdistance the competition with yet another kind of act.

Black stars of the minstrel stage included Bob Height, Horace Weston, James Bland, Lew Johnson, Charles Hicks, Wallace King, James and George Bohee, and Billy Kersands who was the most popular black minstrel of his day.[72] Kersands was such a popular attraction with blacks as well as whites that theater officials suspended the practice of relegating blacks to the galleries and balconies during performances and seated blacks and whites beside each other. As Robert C. Toll states:

> Prejudice was half forgotten as the owners arranged for colored customers to occupy a full half of the theater from the ground floor or orchestra section right up to the gallery with whites filling the other side. [73]

Performing as a minstrel was fraught with danger especially for blacks who challenged the way things were. Traveling on the road at all times of the day and night, in towns all across America, was literally risking one's life. One such story is recounted of a black minstrel, Louis Wright. He and his girlfriend were pelted with snowballs by a group of whites in Missouri. Angry, and probably wanting to appear "manly" in front of his girlfriend, Wright cursed his attackers. They threatened to lynch him for his obstinance and went to the theater where he was performing to make good their threat. Wright, who was armed, fired on the crowd and succeeded in dispersing them. That night, the crowd gathered around the railroad car Wright was traveling in with the other members of his all-black troupe and demanded that he give himself up. When he refused, the entire company was arrested and taken into custody.

BILLY KERSANDS

Billy Kersands was the most popular African-American entertainer of his time. His popularity was similar to that enjoyed by rock stars today.

This drawing shows a stylish African-American entertainer playing the banjo in a minstrel show.

In the middle of the night, Wright was handed over by the sheriff to the waiting mob. He was lynched, his tongue was cut out, and his mutilated body was shipped to his mother in Chicago.[74]

So why did blacks risk life and limb to become minstrels? (1) It was a way out of a life that had few options for blacks during that time. (2) It was one of the few opportunities blacks had for upward mobility from a geographic, economic, and social perspective. (3) It was a chance for them to express their God-given talents and be somebody. (4) Although the black intelligencia did not accept or patronize the minstrel stage as a group, the common people, who attended as often as they could, idolized black performers. They were the matinee idols of their day.

Billy Kersands made $80 a week when the highest paid whites were being paid $75 to $100 a week. Average black minstrels, at the height of their popularity, earned between $10 and $35 dollars a week (an excellent wage compared to what blacks could earn doing manual labor or working in the service industry, which was the normal occupation for most blacks).

*P.G. Lowery's Band and Minstrels were an African-American group
that performed with the Ringling Brothers & Barnum & Bailey Circus. African-American bands,
such as this one, were the first marching bands.*

Even with all of its negatives, "the minstrel show at that time was one of the greatest outlets for talented musicians and artists during that time."[75] It was the minstrel stage that was the proving ground for black entertainers looking to enter the arena of popular culture. It is no accident that many of these performers were more successful on the European stage. James Bland and Bert Williams opted to spend extended periods of time there. Ironically, African-American performers began to enjoy a popularity that was a direct result of the minstrel stage.

As blacks began to express themselves and maintain a balance between their own creativity and the expectations of a fickle audience, they used the opportunity to develop styles of performance that enhanced the field of entertainment in significant ways. They ushered in the concept of the uniformed black marching bands (unheard of before Patrick S. Gilmore during the Civil War),[76] tap dancing, the soft shoe, specialty acts and dances, as well as becoming the proving ground for black composers and a new generation of performers:

> For a long time, then, Negroes played and sang not as they had originally done but as they were supposed to. This was inevitably a period of decadence for both Negro music and American music. For when popular music becomes cut off from sound roots in folk music, and good music has to wall itself about to keep from being contaminated by popular music, music is in a precarious condition all round. This was the situation in American music, with few exceptions, in the period between 1875–1895.[77]

The one casualty would be the banjo. It would never fully recover from the stigma, shame, and humiliation that it created by helping to introduce the "plantation darky" to the world.

CHAPTER TWO

African-American Music 1900 to the Present

The first half of the twentieth century was a turbulent era for African-Americans. They were not yet free, and certainly not slaves. Before the end of the nineteenth century, in the *Plessy versus Ferguson* case the Supreme Court declared that segregation of blacks and whites was legal. The law was a direct affront to the Fourteenth Amendment, which guarantees all citizens (including newly freed blacks), equal protection under the law. The case permitted states to institute racially separate public facilities. The Court decision helped establish a belief within the white community that segregation of the races was not only okay but lawful.

Many whites were still upset by the emancipation of African-Americans. They were afraid that their jobs, communities, and way of life would forever change. They showed their aversion for African-Americans by engaging in lynchings, cross-burnings, intimidation, and other overt and violent acts of racism, particularly in the South. It was this kind of intimidation, on the heels of emancipation, that would continually frustrate and bewilder the African-American community.

Even though African-Americans tried to become independent and useful citizens, they were discouraged at every hand. Lack of educational opportunities and low paying jobs that kept them dependent on whites for their livelihood were constant and oppressive realities. As a result, the desire to be accepted as worthy, contributing, and respected American citizens, and the need to earn a living and provide for their families, was profound. It was this need for survival, especially during the first half of the twentieth century, that had lasting and significant influence on the development of black music and the eventual decline of the black banjo tradition.

Lynching in America

The fate of Louis Wright mentioned previously was by no means unique for African-Americans during the last quarter of the nineteenth century and the first quarter or the twentieth century, especially those who traveled the entertainment circuit. The famous African-American composer W.C. Handy also managed his own minstrel troupe. In the 1890s one of his performers contracted smallpox. The entire troupe was quarantined in a compound and told if they left, they would be lynched. They were further instructed that, if an outbreak of smallpox occurred in one other member of the troupe, they would all be lynched. They were denied food, water, and sanitation facilities. Had it not been for the fact that they carried extra water and food along with them, they would have perished. To escape the town, they dressed fourteen of the sick men in women's clothes and staged their escape to a hospital, fresh food, and humane accommodations.[78]

If one were to think of the most humiliating, violent and inhumane deed perpetrated on the African-American community during the period of the early twentieth century, it would have to be the auction block and subsequent enslavement of Africans and African-Americans. But running a close second would be 3,220 African-Americans who were lynched during the late nineteenth and early twentieth centuries.

There are few examples that illustrate the lengths to which man will go to engage in acts of violence against his fellow man. As a nation, the legacy of lynching in America was a symptom of a nation torn apart by racism. Reading accounts of the mutilations, burnings, hangings, shootings, and dismemberments that took place during the latter part of the nineteenth, and the beginning of the twentieth century, gives vivid evidence of the state of race relations in the American South and elsewhere. It also shows the lengths to which Southern whites would go to intimidate and control the black population. The reign of terror that spread across the South was ample evidence that Southern whites would not relinquish their way of life—not without a fight. But they would not fight the Northern power structure or a nation weary of the disunity that slavery fomented—they would victimize the victims. They would continue to oppress the oppressed.

Lynching was a Southern obsession. When you think of relations between blacks and whites in the South, it is hard not to conjure up images of barking bloodhounds and white men armed with shotguns chasing black men across swamps, fields, and railroad tracks. It's difficult not to envision anxious mobs torturing, mutilating, gawking, and poking fun at lifeless bodies dangling from the end of a hangman's noose. Although mob violence occurred all over the United States, African-Americans (although the predominate victims) were not the only ones. The oppressed also included Native Americans, Hispanics, and Asians. By the late nineteenth century lynching had become primarily Southern and racially limited to African-Americans.

SOME ARRESTING FACTS:

- In the 1880s eighty-two percent of all lynchings occurred in the South.

- In the South, 3,220 blacks were lynched between 1880 and 1930.

- Eighty-five percent of the lynching victims in the South and border states were black.

- The state of Virginia had the fewest lynchings of any other Southern state—Georgia had the most.

- Blacks could be lynched for "wild talk" which could be anything from preaching about African colonization, encouraging black laborers to demand higher pay, or leaving white employers before their contracts were complete.

- On several occasions lynch mobs executed three victims at once, and a few mobs lynched five victims at a time.

- In Virginia, lynchings began to decline by the 1890s. In Georgia, they began to peak in the 1880s and rose sharply until the 1930s.

- Lynch mobs were not made up of malcontents or "rednecks" out for a thrill. Participants were judges, politicians, and other "solid citizens."

In Macon, Georgia, in 1922, mob participants included the manager of a local hotel, the president of an insurance company, a local merchant, and a city firefighter.

- In Georgia, mobs took forty-four percent of the victims from jails, and seventy-two percent from the hands of the law. In Virginia, they took forty-seven percent of their victims from jails and all of their victims from the custody of law officers.

- In Tocca, Georgia, on June 14, 1915, a mob had to settle for firing hundreds of rounds through the cell door into a victim's body because after taking five hours to get into the jail they couldn't break through the jail cell.

- Mass mobs, despite their size, acted swiftly. In Georgia, they captured and executed more than fifty-three percent of their victims within a day of the alleged crime and more than eighty-five percent within a week. In Virginia, they lynched forty-five percent of their victims within a day and more than seventy-five percent within a week.[79]

Every form of mob—private, posse, and terrorist—occurred in Georgia. Although terrorist mobs and posses were smaller in terms of victims in Georgia, those two types, in most cases, lynched more African-Americans than the total of all mobs in Virginia.

The most frequent form of butchery was burning the body after the victim had been hanged. (James Irwin, from Ocilla, Georgia, who was accused of murdering a white girl, was tortured and burned. But before he died, the mob cut off his fingers and toes, pulled out his teeth with pliers, and repeatedly jabbed him in the mouth with a pointed pole. After castrating him, the mob burned him alive.) Lynching was a dirty, inhuman, and cowardly act indeed.

It is interesting to note that ninety percent of the most barbaric lynchings took place in the state of Georgia. Out of the one hundred-plus minstrel troupes Robert Toll chronicled in his book, thirty-five had "Georgia" as a part of their name.[80]

This has not been an easy topic to discuss (or to read for that matter, I'll bet) but it is an important one. The banjo and its development cannot be fully understood from a social perspective without understanding the world in which its users, and listeners, lived. The reality of lynching was central to the thinking of everyone African-American who traveled anywhere in the South, every day of their lives.[81]

The Turn of the Century and the Banjo

The banjo is considered a folk instrument. But there were active attempts to take it uptown and make it "respectable." People such as Samuel Swain Stewart, and other banjo manufacturers and players, wanted to capitalize on the banjo's popularity during the nineteenth century, but despite their best efforts, it essentially remained a folk instrument.[82]

The banjo was also mentioned in slave narratives compiled during the first half of the twentieth century by the Federal Writers Project. This project was funded by the United States government from 1935 to 1941. Its aim was to hire unemployed writers and put them to work collecting American history through oral narratives. President Franklin Delano Roosevelt was convinced by African-American advisors to include the testimonies of former slaves. Because African-Americans were included, more than two thousand ex-slaves in eighteen states spoke with interviewers about their lives, their work, and their experiences on topics from food, ways to recreation, and music. Many of them mentioned the banjo and its importance to the African-American community.

In February of 1937, Mrs. Fannie Berry, from Petersburg, Virginia, remembered the banjo in gatherings she attended as a girl:

> *Used to go over to de Saunders place fo' dancin'. Musta been hundred slaves over thar, an' they always had de bes' dances. Mos' times fo' de dance dy had Dennis to play de banjer. Gals would put on dey spare dress ef dey had one, an' men would put a clean shirt on. Gals always tried to fix up fo' partyin', even ef dey ain't got nothin' but a piece of ribbon to tie in dey hair.* [83]

Marrinda Jane Singleton, born in 1840 in Hartford, North Carolina, also remembered the banjo as part of her upbringing:

> *Evenings after work slaves were allowed to visit each other. Molasses candy pulls, quiltin' and maybe a little dancin' by de tune of an old banjo.* [84]

The banjo was not just a solo instrument. It was accompanied by other instruments as well. If a good time was needed, the banjo was there to oblige. Many ex-slaves talked about the need for relief from the stresses of the day, and how the banjo provided a brief respite from the toils and cares of the day. Nancy Williams of Lahore, Virginia, remembered well:

*Taken during the Civil War, this photo shows slaves
in front of their cabin. Many years later, former slaves provided
narrative accounts of their experiences.*

*Guess I didn' know no better den. Anyhow we'd go to dese dances; ev'y gal had a beau.
An' sech music! You had two fiddles, two tambourines, two bango, an' two sets o' bones.
Dem deblish boys 'ud go out'n de wood an' git de bones whar de cows done died. Yessuh
I'se out dere in the middle o' de flo' jus' a-dancin'; me and Jennie, an' de devil. Dancin'
wid a glass o' water on my head an' three boys a-bettin on me. I hada grea' big reaf
roun' my head an' a big ribbon bow on each side an' didn't wase a drap o' water on
neider. We danced old Jennie down. Me'n de debil won dat night.* [85]

The Rise of African-American Folk Music

Toward the latter part of the nineteenth century, just as minstrelsy was reaching its peak, many white schools of music were formed. Most were dedicated to the training of professional musicians. They included the Peabody Conservatory in Baltimore (1857), the Oberlin School of Music (1865); the New England Conservatory of Music, the Cincinnati Conservatory and the Chicago Musical College, all in 1867; the Philadelphia Musical Academy (1870); the New York College of Music (1878); the National Conservatory of Music at New York (1885); the American Conservatory at Chicago (1886), and the Institute of Musical Art, founded in New York in 1904.[86]

It is no accident that around the turn of the century, symphony orchestras and major opera companies were established as a result of these professional schools (and no doubt, an interest in expressing a more refined and cultured music than what was being touted in American popular culture). They include the Boston Symphony Orchestra (1881), the Philadelphia Orchestra (1900), the Minneapolis Symphony (1903), the Chicago Symphony (1891), and the Cincinnati Symphony (1909).

At least three of the instructors at these schools taught and inspired black composers. Among those composers was William Grant Still, who is considered to be the "Dean of Afro-American Composers."[87] But it was not until 1890 that a school dedicated itself to focusing on American music. That was the year Antonin Dvorák began working seriously on music from the African-American and Native American cultures. His reasoning:

> *These beautiful and varied themes are the product of the soil. They are American. They are the folksongs of America, and your composers must turn to them. In the Negro melodies of America I discover all that is needed for a great and noble school of music.*[88]

Dvořák returned to his native Bohemia in 1895, however, he had awakened an interest in African-American folk music. This interest would spawn the performance of Negro spirituals, rhapsodies, and other symphonic works with black themes.

As a result of this influence, black composers consistently turned to the folk music of their community for inspiration. These composers included Harry T. Burleigh (1866–1949), Clarence Cameron White (1880–1960), R. Nathaniel Dett (1882–1943), John Wesley Work II (1873–1925), Will Marion Cook (1869–1944), and the wonderfully prolific team of Robert Cole (1868–1911), J. Rosamond Johnson (1873–1954), and James Weldon Johnson (1871–1938). It was the Johnson brothers' composition, "Lift Every Voice and Sing," that became known as the Negro National Anthem. Cole and the Johnsons also wrote a work called the "Evolution of Ragtime" in 1903 that had as one of its song titles, "The Spirit of the Banjo." [89]

Ragtime and Blues

Ragtime evolved during the late nineteenth century and was a direct result of the music of black America and the vestiges of the minstrel stage. For about two decades, middle-class whites bought sheet music, listened to, and entertained themselves with a new music that was being played on a relatively new instrument, especially in popular culture, the piano. A by-product of the piano's popularity was the development of sheet music that could be played on piano rolls by player pianos. People who wanted to enjoy piano music—but didn't have the skill to play—could purchase a player piano. These types of pianos could play music automatically with the aid of the piano roll, which was printed music transferred to a roll of paper as perforations. The paper slowly unwound at a speed controlled by the operator who pumped the piano's foot pedals. Pockets of air pushed through a bellows attached to the piano. The perforations

This photo shows the sheet music for a rag called
"The Demon Rag." Ragtime often was used as dance music for such
dances as the cakewalk and slow drag.

and air combined to trigger lifters that caused the hammers of the piano to strike the correct string. As the hammers hit the notes, the piano began to play.[90] This invention made new music accessible to lots of people. The difficulty of playing ragtime made this invention a blessing to many who would not have been able to enjoy the music of the period in the comfort of their own homes.

The main ingredient of piano-rag music, also call "jig piano," was syncopation. The music was an outgrowth of dance-music practices in the black community. During slavery, men and women danced to the music of fiddles and banjos. Percussion and rhythm, so important to dance music in creating a

Probably the most important African-American ragtime composer, Scott Joplin wrote a ragtime classic called "The Maple Leaf Rag." He wrote dozens of rags and a ragtime opera, The Guest of Honor.

sense of time, and especially African-American dance, was done with the feet and hands. With the banjo, additional percussion was provided by strumming and thumping the head as done in the "old time" or "claw-hammer" style of playing which still exists today. In ragtime piano music, percussion was provided with the left hand. The right hand performed the syncopated melodies. So the development of ragtime could not have existed without the influence of the fiddle, and most importantly the banjo, which combined elements of percussion as well as melody.

The ragtime banjo tradition was exemplified in the work of virtuoso banjoists such as Vess L. Ossman, Harry Reser, Phil Russell, and particularly Fred Van Eps. This period (1890–1920) was known as the classic jazz period when the role of the banjo was as a chordal instrument.[91]

Johnny St. Cyr, who played for Louis Armstrong's Hot 5 and Hot 7 groups, played solos and actually accompanied the piano player with his banjo, keeping a steady and dynamic beat throughout the duet.[92] He played the six-string banjo-guitar as well as the tenor banjo. According to Alyn Shipton in *The New Grove Dictionary of Jazz*, St. Cyr and Ikey Robinson "managed to provide propulsion and achieve a sense of swing in a drum-less rhythm section without the clanking monotony obtained by banjoists in later styles of traditional jazz." Other important banjo instrumentalists include William Penn, Emanuel Sayles, Bill Johnson (who played with King Oliver), John Marrero, and Ikey Robinson also known as "Banjo Joe."[93]

Blues musicians were really informal collectors, historians, and storytellers of African-American history. The blues had a symbiotic and organic relationship to black life. Whether the song was a personal statement about relationship gone wrong or an opportunity missed, or a comment on the larger society, it gave voice to African-American hopes, anxieties, fears, frustrations, and longings. It is considered one of the most important genres of music to emerge out of the American social community of the last century. It is not only a musical expression but also a social expression.

During the early twentieth century, there were four primary regions of the country, all of which were heavily populated by African-Americans: the Mississippi Delta, Piedmont Virginia, east Texas, and later New Orleans. Guitarists, such as Charlie Patton, Robert Johnson, and Son House, represented the Mississippi Delta blues.

The nineteenth-century songster tradition, singing and accompanying oneself on the banjo, was represented by Papa Charlie Jackson and principally Gus

*In the 1920s, one of the great jazz bands was
King Oliver's Creole Jazz Band. King Oliver (third from left)
and Louis Armstrong (fourth from left) played the coronet.*

Cannon. Cannon, a banjo player, bridged the gap between the string band tradition and the country blues. In the Piedmont area, which included areas in eastern Virginia into the Carolinas and down to Georgia, musicians such as Josh White were popular. In eastern Texas, and parts of Louisiana, players such as Huddie Leadbelly and Sam Hopkins led the way. New Orleans began a unique style that had its origins in ragtime, minstrel music, and circus marching bands with heavy Creole influences, as exemplified by musicians such as Joseph "King" Oliver and Ferdinand "Jelly Roll" Morton. This New Orleans style of music was seen as different from the "rural" blues that came out of the first three traditions.

The blues was the logical antecedent of the mournful songs of the stevedores, roustabouts, and former slave field hollars, as well as the sorrow songs that were such a part of black spirituals. By singing and playing a song about the fickleness of women or the leaving of a loved one, the singer could have been singing to someone or just commiserating alone with none but the trees to listen. Listeners empathize with the singers and recognize that they not only speak for their personal experiences, but those of the listeners as well.

W.C. Handy (1873–1958) is considered by many as the "Father of the Blues." He certainly was the first man to popularize the genre. When Handy published his "Memphis Blues" in 1912, it was an immediate success. Handy wrote it to support a mayoral candidate, Edward H. Crump, in a Memphis election in 1909. Its first performance was an unqualified success. The members of Handy's band went wild (even when they rehearsed it) and so did the crowd as they listened:

> *People danced on the streets; in the office buildings the "white folks pricked up their ears" and "stenographers danced with their bosses." As a result of this performance Handy's band jumped to the top spot among Memphis bands.* [94]

Some of the African-American string bands such as Gus Cannon's "Jug Stompers" and others had been a part of starting the tradition, but the blues was really a child of the guitar and it expressed the nuance in ways the banjo was not able to. As the guitar became more affordable to rural and low-income blacks, it quickly eclipsed the banjo and became the instrument of choice. By the early twentieth century, the banjo had begun to fade in popularity among African-Americans, and had become extremely popular among whites, especially

Slaves, such as Scipio, were expected to carry out work demanded by plantation owners.
Here, household slaves wait on plantation folk.

care of himself and he knew how to use the white man's ways to his advantage. How else could he have successfully run away three times? He knew where to go, and how to get there. He knew who to talk to and who to avoid. Even though he was not a master of the language, he obviously knew enough to move from one place to the other safely. To walk from Maryland to Philadelphia would take approximately twenty-six hours.[100] A lot could happen in that time. He could be taken up by someone and resold into slavery. He could have been stolen and enslaved by others, as he finally was.

Contrary to reality, artists often portrayed plantation life as a good existence for slaves. This painting shows slaves dancing in the yard of their nicely furnished house. Most slaves really lived in shacks on plantation grounds or in attics or closets of their owners' homes.

His banjo playing must have been special because it was mentioned each time advertisements were taken out for his return. The advertisers knew that banjo players were popular and that, if they were good, they would be playing for large gatherings of people. Like other banjo players in the area, he probably played for black and white audiences.

When he played for African-Americans he might have played to the rhythm of "Juba." This was a type of rhythmic hand patting that used the hands (sometimes one, sometimes both) to slap various parts of the body (head, face, chest, thighs, shoulders, etc.) to keep cadence, much like a drum would, but using more complex and syncopated rhythm patterns. Such a partnership between the banjo and "Patting Juba" was mentioned (much later) in nearby Prince Edward County, Virginia. The hand patting was accompanied by a song the performers sang as they synchronized their rhythm with the notes of the banjo.

Juber up and Juber down,
Juber all around de town,
Juber dis, and Juber dat,
And Juber roun' the simmon vat.
   Hoe corn, hill tobacco,
   Get over double trouble, Juber boys, Juber.
Uncle Phil, he went to mill,
He suck do sow, he starve de pig,
Eat the simmon, gi' me de seed,
I told him, I was not in need.
   Hoe corn! Hill tobacco!
   Get over double trouble, Juber boys, Juber.
Aunt Kate? Look on the high shelf,
Take down the husky dumplin,
I'll eat it wi'my simmon cake.
To cure the rotten belly-ache.
   Hoe corn! Hill tobacco!
   Get over double trouble, Juber boys, Juber.
Racoon went to simmon town,
To choose the rotten from do soun,
Dare he sot upon a sill,
Eating of a whip-poor-will.
   Hoe corn! Hill tobacco!
   Get over double trouble, Juber boys, Juber. [101]

Once in Philadelphia, Scipio had to find food, shelter, clothing, and most of all, safety. Constables, bounty hunters (also known in the African-American community as "Paddy Rollers" or "Patter Rollers"), and anyone looking to make a quick buck, would be out looking for him hoping to collect the reward for his capture. He had to know who to trust and who to doubt, both black and white. He had to know how to get himself out of sticky situations, and explain why he was out by himself beyond the control of his master.

In the eighteenth century, enslaved Africans were not allowed to be out alone without some sort of note or pass (permission slip) from their owners explaining why they were by themselves. This is probably why Scipio on at least two occasions tried to pass himself off as a free man. Scipio had to play a role. He had to convince those around him that he belonged in Philadelphia; that he knew the streets, the stores and other places of interest. Scipio also (probably illegally) acquired a pass indicating that he was free. Many African-American runaways forged or obtained "free papers" (written proof, from their owners, that they were free and not enslaved). If Scipio couldn't convince authorities (literally anyone white) who he was, or why he was traveling alone, he would be treated as a runaway, and since an African-American could not testify against a white person in a court of law, he had no legal recourse. Further, if Scipio was captured by a white person claiming to be his owner, he could be enslaved again.

Scipio could play that banjo and he knew that made him different from most slaves without such skills. He knew whites, as well as African-Americans, wanted to have a good time and (for the price of clothing, shelter, food, or money) he could provide that with his banjo. He probably knew that if he wanted to make his way as a musician he had to play a variety of music. He had to be able to play jigs, reels, and other popular dances of the time. He knew that his banjo could be the difference between being treated well and being treated horribly.

Slaves who ran away knew that they faced severe punishment if caught.
They could be beaten or killed. Some owners
used blazing hot irons to put brands on their runaway slaves.

Scipio also knew it was important to dress well. He certainly couldn't look like a runaway. He had to look like he was a free African-American, like he was special. He had to talk, act, and dress like he was different from the common perception of a plantation slave. The ads described his dress: He wore "a blue broad cloth coat, or a black ditto, old shoes, and stockings." [102]

Even with all he must have known, it was not enough. Eight years after he ran away the first time, he was living with yet another white man from Kent County, Maryland. He ran away from him as well and headed, once again, for Philadelphia! While it is certain his masters wanted him back (even the one who

*African-American banjo players, such as Scipio, often found
work as entertainers for wealthy whites.*

had little success in keeping him, Marcus Kuhl), there must have been something else in Philadelphia that motivated Scipio to keep returning there.
Without a doubt he had friends, perhaps family, a loved one, or simply acquain-
tances he wanted to stay close to. Clearly there was something in Philadelphia
that made him feel it was the place for him to be. But this time it wasn't just his
banjo that he was peddling. In 1757, he was passing himself off as a hatter
(maker of hats). He was still known as a banjoist, but there was something he
now understood about being a skilled craftsmen as well. Such an occupation
offered him even greater legitimacy. [103]

Not much else is known about Scipio. His entire life is chronicled in a few newspaper ads that were never meant to tell us anything about his life, what was important to him, or what he valued as a musician or as a person. He was a slave—a non-person; a labor-saving device that was meant to serve the needs of someone else. But Scipio knew there was something else to life, something more for him than tending to the whims of others. As a result he took his banjo, his dreams, his knowledge of his captors and he exercised the only option he had: he freed himself. There were many banjo players during the eighteenth century, among them Jack, Charles, Billy Banjo, Dadda Gumbo, and many others.[104] They all used the heritage of their culture and their understanding of the banjo as a method of music-making and their understanding of how to play it, and a will to have a life that enslavement denied them.

Horace Weston (1825–1890)

The most popular professional African-American banjoist between 1870 to 1880 was Horace Weston. His career was spent balancing between professional skill and socially restrictive racial stereotyping.[105] He was the son of a free black Connecticut dancing teacher and musician. He played the accordion, violin, cello, double bass, trombone, and guitar. He played these before he took up the banjo.

During the Civil War Weston was in the Navy and carried the banjo with him. He toured the United States, England, France, and Germany with minstrel troupes, *Uncle Tom's Cabin* shows, and Barnum and Bailey Circus. Thirty minutes of showtime was set aside for his playing. His wife also played and sometimes accompanied him. Although he could read music, he played banjo by ear. Because of his talent, where he was born, and what he achieved, he was considered an anomaly—more a freak of nature than a credible representation of African-American talent and intelligence. However, Weston was one of the few African-

Horace Weston was the best-known banjo player of his time. In the 1870s, he performed with the Ringling Brothers & Barnum & Bailey Circus.

American musicians who, despite his race, gained the respect of the white community with his playing ability.

Weston broke many of the stereotypes held about blacks and the banjo. He was seen as a banjoist of the highest order, even in the face of a perception of blacks as plantation darkies who were ignorant, comical, shallow, and "folksy."

His life was spent balancing between his extremely fine talent as a professional musician and the racist community in which he lived. It was a world that relegated him to second class citizenship and thus below the standards of acceptability, no matter how extraordinary his talent.

Ironically, it was Weston's extraordinary depth of talent that allowed him some separation from the rest of his community. He was the headliner in many of the performances he did between 1870 and 1880 and enjoyed a notoriety that most of his African-American contemporaries did not. When Weston died in May of 1890, the New York *Morning Journal* acknowledged his passing and his talent:

> *Weston was, perhaps, the greatest banjoist the world has ever heard. He did not learn on Southern plantations the magic touch that drew the witchery from the strings. He was born of free parents in the Nutmeg State of Connecticut in 1825. . . . He traveled all over the world, and his cleverness on the banjo delighted and astonished people in all parts of the globe.* [106]

Like his contemporary, Paul Laurence Dunbar, Weston was seen as singularly different and apart from the "traditional" Southern African-American. This was not a "darky" who played his banjo in front of a plantation cabin. He did not just play simple melodies. He was a freeborn, sophisticated, educated Yankee from Connecticut. His skill at playing the banjo, his Northern roots, his privileged upbringing (when compared to most blacks of the period) all added justification to the perception that he was more unlike his countrymen than similar to them. He had been influenced by a white society who readily took credit for influencing him beyond the strictures and boundaries of his unfortunate heritage.

James Bland (1854–1911)

Bland was called the "Negro Stephen Foster." He called himself the "best Ethiopian song writer in the world." He was the first African-American recognized for making a noteworthy contribution to American popular music.

Bland was born after slavery and before freedom, at a time when African-Americans, who had just been freed, struggled for every ounce of respect they received. He was the descendant of free blacks.

He was born in Flushing, New York, on October 22, 1854, seven years before the Civil War, in a place where slavery had long since been abolished. His family moved from there to Philadelphia. It was there at the age of twelve that he was to find his passion. One day as he was strolling down the dirt-covered streets of Philadelphia, he came upon an old black man playing the banjo. Although he had never seen or heard such an instrument before, its sound fascinated him. He saw a banjo like the one the man was playing in a local pawn shop. He eagerly awaited his father's return home from work that day so that he could ask him to buy it for him. Because his family was poor, and his father was not able to spend the eight dollars that the instrument cost, James Bland set out to make one of his own. After some time, he had made a crude-looking banjo.

As Bland sat on a porch not far from where he lived, he began playing the first notes on his homemade banjo. The neighborhood bully appeared and demanded to see Bland's masterpiece. All of a sudden, without warning, the bully grabbed the instrument away from Bland, threw it to the ground, and stomped on it. Enraged, Bland lashed out at the bully, who was spoiling for a fight and was twice Bland's size. Although the smaller Bland put forth a gallant effort, he was not able to overpower the bully.

Bruised and ragged from his fight, Bland struggled home and explained to his mother what had happened. Instead of punishing him for fighting, his mother told him how proud she was of him for standing up for himself. That night she

THE BEST ETHIOPIAN SONG WRITER IN THE WORLD

James Bland billed himself as
"The Best Ethiopian Song Writer in the World."

told Bland's father what had happened. Because of his courage, they decided that as soon as they were able, they would purchase a banjo for young James.

In time the family moved to Washington, D.C. where Bland's father was appointed the first African-American examiner in the U.S. Patent Office. They lived very close to the newly opened Howard University where Bland's father enrolled to study law around 1868. James worked as a page in the House of Representatives, which qualified him for membership in the Manhattan Club. The club was made up of African-American clerks who worked for the Federal government. He even formed a glee club with other members and entertained visitors to the nation's capital as well as prominent citizens of the city.[107]

In the early 1870s, James saw the famous white minstrel George Primrose perform. As a result, James set out to become an entertainer. He left Howard University without graduating and set out to follow his dream. Ironically, because of his race, he could not readily find work as a minstrel because all minstrel performers were white males. It would take him three years to obtain his first paying job as a minstrel.

By now Bland was of college age and his father felt it was time he began to think about what he wanted to do with his life. Bland and his father had many arguments about what would be his life's work. Bland wanted to be an entertainer, but his father, being a member of the enlightened and educated Negro intelligentsia (educated black elite), had other plans for his son. During this period blacks were trying to lift themselves out of the poverty and ignorance that slavery perpetuated. Many African-Americans, especially the famous African-American scholar W.E.B Du Bois, felt that their future depended on the small number of blacks who had managed to get an education. This group of gifted people were referred to as the "Negro intelligentsia" or the "talented tenth."

It is our duty then, not drastically but persistently, to seek out colored children of ability and genius, to open up to them broader, industrial opportunity and above all, to find that Talented Tenth and encourage it by the best and most exhaustive training in order to supply the Negro race and the world with leaders, thinkers, and artists. [108]

Life for newly emancipated blacks in the 1870s and '80s was difficult to say the least. A new white terrorist organization, the Ku Klux Klan, was spreading hate and fear all across the South and their primary targets were newly freed blacks. Jim Crow laws relegated blacks to second class citizenship. They could not get decent jobs, wages, education, or anything that allowed them to help themselves.

The senior Bland saw the answer in education and scholarship. For him, his son's desire to play the banjo and be an entertainer was irresponsible and played right into the hands of those who wanted to continue oppressing and stereotyping his people.

Many times the only way Bland and his father could talk to one another was through the mediation of Bland's mother. She tried to convince the elder Bland that maybe James would someday become as famous with his God-given gift as his father had with his.

In the nineteenth century the most popular entertainment was minstrel shows. They were as popular back then as going to the movies is for us today.

In minstrel shows, African-Americans were portrayed as lazy, shiftless slackers who cared only about the pleasures of the moment. They were shown as always loving watermelons and were always raiding a melon patch.

They were further stereotyped as being experts with a razor. Folk legend had it that skilled blacks could throw an apple in the air and slice it into four even pieces before it hit the ground. And shooting craps (a game that used dice for gambling) was another of their favorite pastimes, according to those who portrayed the lives of plantation blacks.

According to minstrel performers, the average African-American man had an unusually large mouth, thick lips, bulging eyes, and a broad grin that exposed

*It was blackface minstrel entertainers like this one who convinced Bland
that he should become a minstrel himself. Blackface minstrels often dressed in
formal clothing and used exaggerated language in a parody of African-Americans.*

pearly white teeth. He dressed in gaudy colors and in a flashy style. He usually drank more gin than he could handle, and loved chickens so well that he could not pass a chicken coop without stealing one.

On the minstrel stage the African-American man's love for being the dandy was combined with his attempts to use big words. These were so long, with so many syllables that he could not possibly understand their meaning, so he twisted the syllables in the most ludicrous ways in his primitive efforts to pronounce them.

This then, is what the elder Bland, Howard University, and most of the "Negro intelligentsia" of the day were fighting against. They wanted to tear down stereotypes they felt endangered any chances of full citizenship. To them, the banjo was a symbol of slavery, oppression, shame, disgrace, humiliation, and emasculation. It reminded them of a time and a lifestyle they could no longer afford to endure—a lifestyle they desperately wanted to forget.

As stated earlier, Bland attended Howard University (his father had enrolled in Howard's law school), though we have no evidence he graduated. He did spend a great deal of time on campus listening to the stories and songs of the laborers who worked there. Most of them had been slaves. He was moved by their spirituals, their rhythms, and their harmony. He also got into trouble with campus officials for trying to start a minstrel troupe on campus. This was frowned on by the administration.

While at Howard, James met a girl named Mannie Friend. She was infatuated with Bland and loved his banjo playing and singing. On afternoons after classes they would stroll along the streets of Washington, D.C. and he would play his banjo for her.

One day as they were walking along, an elderly black man stopped to listen to Bland play his banjo. After listening for a few minutes, he asked Bland where he had picked up the song he was playing. Bland told him it was an original. He then asked Bland to follow him to his studio. He was a musician himself, and he saw a potential in Bland that surpassed his own. He offered to teach him music theory and so, for a time, Bland studied under the "Professor" (no other name is available).[109]

As James and Mannie continued to spend time together, she told him about her home in Tidewater, Virginia and how she missed it while attending Howard. She described the land, the people, and the atmosphere of her hometown so vividly that it intrigued Bland and he asked her if she would take him there. She lived on a plantation just outside of Williamsburg, called the Smith Plantation.

Word had been sent to her that the black overseer (John MacGregor) from the plantation would be coming to Washington to deliver a load of tobacco and that she, and her new friend, could ride back with him. It took three days to get to Tidewater from the nation's capital.

As Bland rode in the wagon with Mannie and the overseer, he saw wondrous sights. He saw rivers and streams teaming with fish and other wildlife. He saw magnolia, cypress, and sycamore trees swaying in the breeze. He saw deer, fox, raccoons, and squirrels. He saw hills and mountains and then, finally, the shores of the James and York rivers. Everywhere James went there was peace and quiet. He was so struck by it all, that he said very little to Mannie as they drove along.

The Smith Plantation was right on the edge of the James River and one night during their visit, as he and Mannie sat under a cypress tree, Bland began to transform his thoughts and emotions into music and song:

Carry me back to old Virginny,
There's where the cotton and the corn and taters grow,
There's where the birds warble sweet in the spring-time
There's where this old darky's heart am long'd to go.

There's where I labored so hard for old Massa,
Day after day in the field of yellow corn;
No place on earth do I love more sincerely
Than old Virginny, the state where I was born.

Sung with Great Success by Alma Gluck

Carry me Back to Old Virginny

Song and Chorus

by

James A. Bland

50

Boston-Oliver Ditson Company

NewYork-Chas.H.Ditson & Co. ☞ ☞ ☞ ☞ Chicago-Lyon & Healy

The sheet music for Bland's most famous song showed a scene
of Southern African–American life with a banjo player. Until recently,
his composition was the official song for the state of Virginia.

Carry me back to old Virginny,
There let me live till I wither and decay.
Long by the old dismal swamp have I wandered,
There's where this old darky's life will pass away.

Massa and missis have long since gone before me,
Soon we will meet on that bright and golden shore,
There we'll be happy and free from all sorrow,
There's where we'll meet and we'll never part no more. [110]

It was that song which so impressed the lead performer (George Primrose) in the most popular minstrel troupe of the day, Haverly's Minstrels, that he used it in their repertoire. It was that song that established Bland as a serious composer, the likes of Stephen Foster. It was that song that launched him on a career that would earn him the sponsorship of William Lloyd Garrison, Oliver Wendell Holmes, James Russell Lowell, and P. T. Barnum.

In 1881, Bland toured England with the all-black Calender-Haverly minstrel troupe. A few months later when the group was to return to America, Bland and a few others decided to stay. They knew, like many African-American performers of the day, that they would be more welcome and respected for their talents in Europe than they could ever expect in America.

Bland played his own compositions all over Europe, including England, Scotland, and Germany where his popularity rivaled that of Stephen Foster and John Philip Sousa. He even gave a command performance for Queen Victoria and the Prince of Wales.

It was during those years (1878–1900) that Bland enjoyed a salary of $10,000 a year, plus royalties from his compositions.[111] But like most blacks during the period, Bland did not copyright the bulk of his compositions. Although it is believed that he composed more than six hundred songs, the Library of Congress records only fifty-three. However his popularity as a composer

The popular Minstrel Book *included white entertainers in blackface makeup on the cover and jokes, poems, and songs inside.*

was acknowledged wherever he traveled in Europe. He was known as "the Prince of Negro songwriters." [112]

Bland's success as a performer was also legendary. He is said to have had a specialty that involved singing, dancing, and acrobatic stunts while playing the banjo. Known for his comedy, he was billed as the "Idol of the Music Halls." [113]

At one of his performances, an Englishman remarked:

> *I heard a humorous balladist not long since, a minstrel with wool on his head, and an ultra Ethiopian complexion, who performed a Negro ballad that I confess moistened these spectacles in a most unexpected manner. I have gazed at thousands of tragedy queens dying on the stage and expiring in appropriate blank verse, and I never wanted to wipe them. They have looked up, be it said, at many scores of clergymen, without being dimmed, and behold! A vagabond with a corked face and a banjo sings a little song, strikes a wild note, which sets the heart thrilling with happy pity.* [114]

Such was the lure of the minstrel stage when done well. It is said that Bland was able to capture more of the poignancy, the lyric mood, the rhythmic pulse, and the unique sense of time, place, and condition of his people than Stephen Foster could ever imagine. Yet Bland never received the recognition that Foster enjoyed.

In 1901, the minstrel stage was in decline. Musical theater and vaudeville were replacing minstrelsy and Bland could no longer make a living. Because he did not use his money wisely, he returned to America penniless. He managed to get a low-paying job, and even wrote a stage musical, *The Sporting Girl,* which was a box office flop. His day had come and gone. He eventually moved to Philadelphia where, destitute and ill, he died of tuberculosis on May 5, 1911.

In 1940 the state of Virginia paid Bland the ultimate compliment and adopted "Carry Me Back to Old Virginny" as the official state song. In 1946 his gravestone was found and rededicated at Merion Cemetery outside Philadelphia, Pennsylvania, where it still is today. The governor of Virginia and W.C. Handy were among the important people who paid homage to the Ethiopian Minstrel. He was finally recognized and given a modicum of the recognition he so deserved, thirty-five years after his death.

On February 18, 1997, the Virginia House of Delegates voted 100–0 to retire the state song, "Carry Me Back to Old Virginny." Many people, both black

Although he never received the recognition he deserved, Bland was a superb entertainer and song writer.

and white, felt the song was too racially offensive to be a symbol of pride for all Virginians. For many, the song represented a racially charged period in the life of the United States that is too painful to serve as the symbol of a state about to enter the twenty-first century. Ironically, the effort to have the song removed was championed by L. Douglass Wilder, the first African-American governor of Virginia since Reconstruction.

James Bland's name has been obscured and almost forgotten. It is doubtful that his musical contributions will ever shake the stigma that the period he lived in represented. Robert C. Toll in *Blacking Up* said of Bland's compositions:

His nostalgic Old Darkies expressed great love for their masters and mistresses; his plantation songs were free from antislavery protests and from praise of freedom; his religious songs contained many stereotyped images of flashy dressers and overindulgent parties; and his Northern Negroes strutted, sang, danced, and had flapping ears, huge feet and gaping mouths. [115]

Rather than becoming part of the freedom generation, Bland opted for a life that was true to his passion as an artist. He gave the audiences what they wanted and they loved him for it. His ultimate success as an individual was his ultimate failure as a representative of his race.

Bland teetered between two worlds: the world of his father's that sought to define new structures of African-American identity, which insured justice and equality, and the world his heart yearned for. But he could not have that world without paying the price of the shame it brought to those of his race who felt that the good of the culture outweighed the good of the individual. His struggle to find his own way was never realized in the land of his birth, but his contributions are worthy of our attention and our respect.

Gus Cannon (1883–1979)

Gus Cannon was born in Marshall County, Mississippi, on September 12, 1883, to a poor, sharecropping family. His family lived on the Henderson Newell Plantation in Red Banks, Mississippi.

Barely eighteen years after the emancipation of African-Americans, the South was experiencing the difficulties of having to welcome and accommodate a newly enfranchised population of citizens who were eagerly awaiting all of the benefits of being American. But in Red Banks, just as in most other places in the South, African-American emancipation did not guarantee all the advantages of the democracy mentioned in the Constitution and Bill of Rights.

*This photo shows the young Gus Cannon with his banjo,
an instrument that was never very far away from him.*

At the end of the Civil War, freed African-Americans had been promised forty acres and a mule, but most did not get it. As a result, most blacks began their journey as freed men and women, with no education, no land, no jobs, and consequently no way of wresting themselves from the yoke of slavery. They were forced to do in freedom what they had learned to do as slaves: work the land.

With the exception of the railroad, Red Banks was just barely a town: one store, which sold everything from pork chops to Stetson hats; a few cafes that featured dancing in the front and dice games in the rear; and a post office which was closed most of the time.

Gus's father, John Cannon, was a sad man who remained bitter most of his life because he saw no evidence of the newly acquired freedom that had been given to blacks by the Thirteenth Amendment. All he had witnessed for himself, his wife and nine children, was poverty, dependence, hard work, and broken promises.

The elder Cannon eked out a living for himself and his family by share-cropping. Sharecropping was an economic arrangement between a landowner (usually white) and a tenant (usually black) that leased land, in exchange for a percentage of the crops grown. From the time John's nine children were able to carry a bucket of water from the well, they were expected to become share-croppers and live off the land as best they could.

In addition to sharecropping, Gus's father had learned to grow and harvest herbs from a Cherokee friend. The Native American, also taught him how to use leaves, tree bark, grass, roots, and berries to ward off disease and evil spirits, and how to use them to cure and treat ailments. This form of healing was popular in the deep South during that time. The scarcity of trained doctors, their reluctance to serve minorities, and the sheer expense involved in treatment, made this alternative form of healing popular. The elder Cannon would periodically take those herbs and remedies into town and sell them to local root doctors, conjurers, and herbalists who were interested in the healing arts. This "side business" was a blessing for the elder Cannon. Many times it was the only alternative to a poor crop or lost shares from a bad growing season.

When Gus was six years old, his father took him to Memphis to sell herbs to merchants who made medicine out of them. As they rode down Beale Street, young Gus heard sounds and saw people that fascinated him. Beale Street was lined with clubs where musicians performed and the music drifted out into the street. It was actually one of the herbalists who told Gus's father what he already knew: "That boy got the gift. He don't need nothing but to be free to follow his heart." [116]

Gus learned very early the kind of tone to use when talking to white people: a tone of obedience and docility; one that was safe and non-confrontational. Unless he wanted to incur the wrath of white people, most of whom were still trying to adjust to being masters without slaves, he had to display a countenance of downcast eyes and a manner of subservience.

The years following the Civil War were very volatile and dangerous for blacks. The Ku Klux Klan, White Citizens Council, and most of the white community still had problems dealing with free blacks who no longer were owned and controlled by them. As a result, thousands of blacks were lynched for the crimes they did not commit, or for something as small as looking at a white woman. Any hint of intelligence, independence, or aggressive behavior of any sort was not only frowned upon but dangerous. Such an attitude could bring more trouble for him and his family than he could handle.

As Gus grew, it was obvious to his parents, especially his father, that he did not want to be a sharecropper, and had no real love for the land. His attention was elsewhere. He wanted to play music. He had trouble concentrating on the work he was assigned to do. At church his mind wandered off. He would let the lard get too hard during soap-making time. He would grind the sausage too soft during hog-killing time. Whatever the work, his heart and soul was not focused on it. He was a dreamer. As his father constantly said, "He was listening to the wind." **117**

During those days, it was thought that each time a musician played a special song and committed it to the wind by performing it, some young person, with a kindred spirit, heard it and committed himself to becoming a bluesman too. Gus had heard these sounds in his head. Sounds of music he could not express. Sometimes he did not even know what it meant, only that it was there, and that it was important.

When Gus expressed this desire to his father, his father did not support such an irresponsible notion, especially from a young black boy who had much more to learn about life. He felt that Gus was better off not listening to the wind, but keeping his feet firmly planted on the ground. Gus needed to learn how to work and take care of himself, and farming was about all he could hope for, and certainly all his father could teach him. After all, many people during that time farmed and played music when they were not working. It was unheard of to think anyone, save a precious few, could make a living playing music.

Gus expressed to his father his love for music and his desire to do that for the rest of his life, but his father understood the difference between "dreaming and doing." He even tried to set Gus up with a sharecropping agreement. But the morning before his father was to set up the agreement with the landowner, Gus ran away.

Like many others Gus left the farm because of the toll it took from his soul. But the farm life never really left him. It was with him when he woke up in the morning and it lulled him to sleep at night. The sounds of music were every-where, but only he could hear it.

"The music was what he knew and he found a way to express all he had ever learned from John Cannon, for his father was all the every day working men which Gus came into contact with. The memories of the dust rising up from the hoofs of the mules and settling in John's hair, turning the kinky wool like cap into a soft brown halo, was settled in Gus's mind. The feel of the dirt turning into clay between Gus's toes as he worked the fields, after many a spring and summer rain, was the sound of music to Gus. The flies resting on the backs of mules, his father flicking them away with the whip and the same man applying a soothing salve to the ears of the animals to relieve the bites of the flies his whip could not reach, was the blues of the Delta to Gus Cannon." [118]

In 1895 Gus made his first banjo. Years later, he wrote:

> When I was twelve years old, one of my brothers (Tom I think) came and got me and took me down to Clarksdale—that's where he lived, South of Clarksdale by Sunflower River. . . . West of Dublin. . . . Hushpuckena. . . . Used to chop cotton there. Yassuh! So that's where I made my first Banjo from a guitar neck and a bread pan mama used to bake biscuits in—had to hold it over fire to tighten up the head before I could play it. [119]

By 1901 he was playing on a new banjo his brother had won in a crap game. "My brother won it in a crap game—put a coon-hide on it." [120] Because it was his first real banjo, he played it every chance he got. When the workday was over, he would head for his banjo and play it for hours.

By now (early 1900s) he could also play a guitar and blow a jug. The jug and the guitar were borrowed instruments. Most of his life he played other people's instruments. When he did have instruments, they spent long stints in pawnshops where he went seeking money during hard times. For a musician with no other visible means of support, there were lots of hard times.

In Clarksdale, he moved from job to job during the day and played music from Friday nights to early Sunday morning. For Gus, as well as most musicians, music was a mistress and a passion, because it was the essence of freedom. When Gus played his music, for just a short while, he was free from the discrimination of the day; free from the responsibilities of manhood; free from the expectations of his father; free from the life he was forced to lead and the world that would not accept him.

Around 1901 his older brothers, Houston and Elmo, searched for and found Gus in Clarksdale. His homemade banjo had been stolen and he was making music playing on an old whiskey bottle. Gus was tired of the life he had been living trying to pursue his music and when he did not have an instrument, he felt it must be time for him to call it quits. Elmo saw a crap game being played on the corner and entered the game. Within minutes he had won a banjo (apparently the second one as a result of a crap game) that he gave to Gus. Gus took that as a sign that he should continue to play his music. His brothers had really come to tell him that his mother and father had died from an illness and had asked for him before they died. However, they decided against telling him because they felt it would only add to his feelings of guilt. They left without telling him.

In 1903 Gus left Clarksdale with his banjo, a small bundle of clothes, and no money. Part of the reason for him leaving was the popularity of W.C. Handy. Handy was the only musician in the region who could read the music he played. He was soon more popular than Gus.

Gus recorded some of his music in Belzoni, Mississippi. However, it was not enough to make him any money, "just enough money to make him bitter against, and distrustful of whites." [121]

Between 1908 and 1912, Gus worked on the Snooks Dillehunt Plantation in Asheport, Tennessee. As always, he worked during the week and, on the weekends, traveled around the area playing music.

In 1913, Gus married his first wife, Bessie. Within two years Bessie died while Gus was on the road against her wishes. He had spent so much of his life as a vagabond, he was not able to adjust to the life of a family man, and he was simply not ready to settle down.

Life as a music man was challenging, but it also had its rewards. Gus had been acquainted with many women and there were people who were fascinated by his talent and wanted to get to know him intimately. Because he was always moving around and searching for the next "gig," it was more difficult for him to establish long-term relationships.

Gus had always enjoyed drinking, but he never fancied hard drugs. "I don't use no dope. . . . no Sir! I drink beer and whisky. . . . oh, I used to be wild about it! Beer keeps me going. I seen so many of them use dope in Memphis, Chicago. . . . oh, don't say nothing! Noah, my harp player, used to be full of coke all the time." [122]

Because he never learned to read or write, he made many mistakes with his money. He was not a good financial manager in general, so he was never able to do much with the money he made.

He also traveled as a hobo, hopping freight trains between Tennessee, Arkansas, Mississippi, and Missouri. He had to be very careful because this was a time of lynching and all manner of violence toward blacks. Any harm that came to a lone, poor, uneducated black man traveling by himself would hardly be noticed by anyone. His only safety was his banjo and his music.

It was at this point that Gus became known as Banjo Joe as he traveled with several medicine shows. During the nineteenth century, these itinerant healers traveled in covered wagons across much of the country (especially the South and in mountain communities) stopping in towns and selling their medicinal cure-alls.

Many people had more faith in him than they had in the "real" doctors. Most saw customers at home or were door to door peddlers, but some, who had the nerve and could afford it, put medicine shows on the road, selling their cure-alls from the back of a truck. To draw crowds some doctors doubled as ventriloquists, magicians, etc.— others employed blackface comedians or a musician, usually blues or country music. The ones who were big-time and had someone backing them, had big tent shows and Pullman buses. [123]

Dr. Stokey (an African-American) was not a real doctor, but he knew a great deal about medicine. He was the first man Gus traveled with. He assisted in mixing potions and selling remedies. The majority of his medicine was colored water and sorghum molasses mixed with lots of whiskey. People who could not afford a real doctor (and many of them black) were eager to obtain these remedies, which represented an amalgam of science, folklore, voodoo, myth, and outright lies.[124]

Traveling with the medicine show, Gus dressed in the finery of the day and flirted with the women as he danced and played music from the stage of the medicine show. He also juggled and told jokes.

Although Gus felt sorry for the poor people who bought the "magic potions" thinking that they would heal their ailments, he never said anything and he went along with the scam. When the minstrel shows came to the South and Midwest, Banjo Joe and the medicine shows became a thing of the past.

By 1918, Gus had come full circle and was working on a farm in Ripley, Tennessee.

When Dr. Miller, another "doctor" he traveled around with, decided to go back on the road again, Gus went with him. He played for the medicine show and performed at fish fries and local parties throughout the South.

While out on one of their trips one day, Miller and Gus, who had not done well selling their remedies on a particular day, found themselves a long way from home and hungry. When they stopped at the first house they saw, an old toothless woman answered the door. They told her they were hungry and asked her if she could spare some food. Her response was, "I got some fat back and biscuits left over from this morning. I be pleased to share it with you. Just walk right in and sit down, I'll soothe your bellies and minds." Cannon never forgot those words and they became the inspiration for his most famous song, "Walk Right In and Sit Right Down."

Around 1928, Gus joined Dr. C. Hankenson's medicine show and traveled

This photo, taken about 1930, shows Cannon's Jug Stompers with
(left to right) Gus Cannon, John Estes, and Noah Lewis.

through North Carolina and Virginia. It did not take him long to tire of this
way of life, so he formed a musical group of his own called the "Jug Stompers."
These medicine men were also musicians, in fact both Elijah Avery (Dr. Stokey)
and Hosea Woods (Dr. Miller) ended up being members of Cannon's band.
RCA Victor Recording had talked with Gus about forming a jug band to add
to their stable of race records (a growing segment of the recording industry that
catered to African-American recording artists and audiences). Gus was only too
happy to oblige.

Gus later made a recording in Chicago. His song "Walk Right In" did very well and was number one on the charts. Unfortunately, because Gus had signed away his right to royalties, he did not receive any money for the thousands of copies that were sold.[125] He soon joined Dr. Streak's medicine show and worked in Alabama and the Gulf Coast area. He even got to work as an extra in a movie called "Hallelujah!" But, as always, he spent his earnings irresponsibly and returned to Beale Street once more.

His years traveling with the "doctor shows" were highlights for him. When he traveled with these shows, it was as if, for a short while, he had the family that always eluded him. Second, it was a wonderful outlet for him to express his talent. He was at his most creative during these improvisational and high-energy moments. "Aw they were the best years I ever had. . . . we was like one big family. If there was a doctor show today I'd be on it."[126]

Around 1940, Gus was getting too old to travel. There was a carnival in Memphis that was taking place on Beale Street. The carnival was run by a Doctor Venson. The activities lasted for several days and included parties, parades, and social events. The elite of the community came out. It reminded Gus of the medicine shows but without the lies. Gus played at the carnival. He also played music at the Peabody Hotel and then traveled to Chicago where he worked in Old Town North. He also played aboard the steamboat, *Memphis Queen.*

His song, "Walk Right In," was a big success and Stax Records was interested. For a few years he lived well in spite of warnings by one of his best friends, Timmy Wilkins, who had become a preacher, that the music they played was becoming a thing of the past. Many places that were popular on Beale Street had either changed or been torn down. Places like Church Park, The Auditorium, Hunt House, Pee Wee's Saloon, The Monarch Room, were no longer there. About the only thing left was A. Schwab, which was a store that sold everything imaginable, including voodoo potions, pamphlets, miracle cures, curses, spell lifting, good luck, and money and love potions. The store sold to both black and white customers. Memphis had grown politically, economically, and socially, but Beale Street by the mid-sixties had not.

By the late 1960s and early '70s, Gus Cannon had become a forgotten man. He was too old to hire out as a farmer, riverboat entertainment was gone, the recording industry was no longer interested in him, the banjo had lost its appeal, especially in the black community, and his style of playing was seen as more "Uncle Tom" than B.B. King. Beale Street had become a place that catered to others, and besides, it was not safe anymore.

When Dr. Martin Luther King, Jr. was killed in 1968, looting, fire, violence and rage overcame the downtown and south-side sections of the city along the river. Beale Street suffered as well. As a result of the unrest and destruction, city officials decided to board up Beale Street, which they perceived as the center of the storm. Buildings were abandoned and most left to decay.

The Roof Tops recorded "Walk Right In and Sit Right Down," but Gus was not given any royalties because he had not written down his music or tried to establish ownership. In addition, he sang it everywhere he could, so other musicians picked it up and claimed it as theirs (a common occurrence during that time).

One day when Gus had gotten some royalties from "Walk Right In" (he received BMI royalties from air play), he went out to buy some beer on Beale Street. On his way home, he was held up in Handy Park. Gus, who had never been robbed in his life, refused to give in. The attackers knocked him to the ground, stomped on his chest and his side. He had a cane with him, and he gave them more of a fight than they were expecting. Although they didn't get his money, they did damage his throat. "I'm still pretty strong. But one of them hit my throat and after that I just can't sing like before. You just can't go out safe these days. I done got old and I'm nervous and I'm scared. Age done got the old man. . . ."[127]

By now, Gus no longer craved the banjo. (Actually he had stopped playing as early as the 1950s for money.) He felt it was bad business and not worth his time anymore. He did odd jobs such as raking yards, cutting lawns and other odd manual jobs. By now his third wife Lela, who had been married to him for a while but was much younger than Gus, was all he had.

He had a few nieces and nephews who came to visit him and gave him money when they could spare it. He played for them when they visited. The banjo was gone, but the jugs were still there, and best of all, they were inexpensive to acquire.

The heyday of Gus Cannon was over. He was now an old man wearing house shoes on swollen feet, for these journey carriers had seen many a mile and the ankles lapped over the sides of the cloth covering. A hat, battered and worn, rode high on his head and covered the fading hairline. A pair of suspenders held up the pants which had belonged to some other man, for they were too short for Gus's legs and too large for his waist. The shirt was a disappearing plaid and several buttons were missing. Gus's eyesight was moving away from the clearness which had once been theirs, but someone had given him a pair of eyeglasses. One of the arms was broken. Gus had taped it together. He no longer shaved and several days of stubble rested on the once charming and elusive face. It was a sad sight, a man who had ridden into Memphis, Tennessee, as a young boy on a wagon which carried natural healing.[128]

By this time the bitterness that Gus felt was at its peak. He blamed white people for everything that was wrong in his life. In an interview to his biographer Bengt Ollson in 1973, Gus made a point of talking about how he had been tricked and duped most of his life. "Everyone's trying to make a buck off the old man. I'm coming and you're going. . . . it's too late for me to get a break."[129]

On October of 1979, Gus was admitted to the Methodist Hospital near downtown Memphis. He died on October 15th. He was 96 years old.[130]

Johnny St. Cyr (1890–1966)

Around the same time Gus Cannon was developing his style of banjo playing in Red Banks, Mississippi, another banjo player, Johnny St. Cyr, was playing jazz in Louisiana. St. Cyr was born in New Orleans, Louisiana on April 17, 1890. Although St. Cyr's father, Gilbert, played guitar and flute, Johnny never heard him play. His parents were separated when he was five years old.[131] St. Cyr began playing the banjo around 1917 while playing on a riverboat in New Orleans.

> *I played with the band on the boat and one of the Strekfus Brothers called me into the office and asked me if I wanted to play with the band regularly. "What are you paying?" I asked. He said, "In New Orleans we are paying $30.00 a week, and when we get to St. Louis we pay $52.50 a week." I said, "I'll try it.". . . I worked 1918, 1919, and 1920 on that boat.* [132]

Like the guitar, the banjo was generally played in the jazz world as a rhythm instrument. Very rarely did you hear a banjo solo. It was a welcome sight in most bands that specialized in dance music. St. Cyr made a banjo-guitar (essentially a banjo that could be strummed and fingered like a six-string guitar) that he played on a riverboat when he signed on in 1918. Shortly after joining, the riverboat sailed to St. Louis. It was there that St. Cyr bought a banjo-guitar made by the Vega Company. The owner of a pool hall had been given the instrument, apparently to settle a debt. He asked St. Cyr to assess the banjo and its worth. St. Cyr did and questioned the owner about purchasing it for himself. He treasured that instrument from the time he bought it (for twenty dollars, ten of which he had to borrow), and played it throughout his life. "This is the instrument that I used on all my recording dates with the Hot 5 in Chicago several years later. I still have it, and play it now and then, when banjo is required on the job. Of course, it has been worked over [overhauled] several times, but it is still with me." [133]

Fate Marables' S. S. Capitol Orchestra featured Johnny St. Cyr (fourth from the left) on the banjo.

Dixieland jazz, the style of music St. Cyr played, is a particular style of jazz, just as "bebop" and "swing" are unique styles. Dixieland jazz is considered by many music scholars to be the earliest form of jazz and New Orleans is the place where it began. From there it spread to Chicago, St. Louis, and other cities.

As early as 1758 New Orleans was acknowledged as a center of African-American music. One of the most popular spots, Congo Square, was a place of assembly for African-American gatherings. In fact thirty years before Johnny St. Cyr was born, Congo Square had become a place for an annual celebration attended by every race and class.

North of Rampart street. . . . is the celebrated Congo Square, well enclosed, contain-ing five or six or perhaps more acres, well shaded, with graveled walks and beautiful grass plats, devoted on Sunday afternoons to negro dances and amusement. . . . The lower order of colored people and negroes, bond and free, assemble in great numbers in Congo Square, on every Sunday afternoon in good weather, to enjoy themselves in their own peculiar manner. Groups of fifties and hundreds may be seen in different sections of the square, with banjos, tom-toms, violins, jawbones, triangles, and various other instruments from which harsh or dulcet sounds may be extracted; and a variety, indeed, of queer, grotesque, fantastic, strange, and merry dancers are to be seen. . . . [134]

The first music St. Cyr remembered hearing was played on a mandolin and a guitar. The instruments were played by Jackie Dowden and Jules Batiste, who called themselves "Jack and Jill." [135] After hearing them play, he got his mother's guitar (she played guitar in only two keys, C and G, and she taught them to him), and went over to the two musicians to ask if he could join them. His play-ing impressed the two musicians and they invited him to play with them.

Fish fries, balls, birthday parties, subscription parties, weddings, anniver-saries, births, and deaths were all occasions where music was played in New Orleans. From small combos of three or four people to full-sized bands of eight to ten musicians, music was all around St. Cyr.

In the very early days the bands played for subscription parties. You subscribed to a party [where those allow to attend had to buy a ticket] and only ticket holders were admitted. This was the way in which they kept out the riff-raff. Of course, there were no radios, movies, or TV in those days—the only forms of entertainment were dances and parties. The bands played for birthday parties, weddings, anniversaries, births and fancy balls, but the "young set" were not allowed to got to the balls unless chaperoned. Lots of them, whose parents did not care for the balls, would give parties in the homes, hence the subscription parties. This was around 1900. [136]

The type of music Johnny St. Cyr played with his banjo was very popular because it was dance music. Dances such as quadrilles,[137] schottisches (a type of circular dance), the waltz, slow drags, one-steps, and two-steps, were being done all over town. Musicians were constantly being hired to entertain.

Unlike other banjo players already discussed, St. Cyr was a musician and not a singer. He did not sing along and play his instrument in solo fashion. In fact, most of his playing was done as a studio musician or with bands in very formal situations. As his skill increased, so did the demand for his talents. St. Cyr played for some of the best bands of his day and with three of the most popular names of his day—Freddie Keppard, Sidney Bechet, and Louis Armstrong. The most famous, Louis Armstrong, used St. Cyr in his band "The Hot 5." St. Cyr met Armstrong through his brother. Armstrong was playing in a small nightclub and St. Cyr went with his brother to hear him.

My brother would go up to Louis, and throw his arms around him and kiss him. This would embarrass Louis and he'd say, "Don't do that, people will think I'm funny."[138]

Most of the bands St. Cyr played with had musical repertoires consisting of thirty or forty songs. Unlike the folk musicians we've discussed, many jazz musicians could read music. The most popular form of music was called "hot playing." This music was very improvisational. Because of the skill needed to play such music, it was only done after the band had formally learned a piece of music—only then could a musician deviate from the theme as written and make up his own. "Hot" music was very popular with the young crowd. Hot playing usually happened in the last chorus of a number. That's when everyone in the band "turned loose" and played their most innovative and creative music. The full range of the musician's skill was showcased during these times.

Like most musicians of his day, St. Cyr had a day job. He was a plasterer. At age fifteen he was apprenticed to a professional plasterer.

St. Cyr was a member (second from left) of Louis Armstrong's "Hot 5" band.

I was apprenticed to the plastering trade about 1905. Working with George Guesnon's father, who was a journeyman plasterer. We worked for August Bon Hagen, a contractor. When I had served out my apprenticeship, I had saved a little money and was able to get out and go to halls and different functions where the bands were playing. [139]

In 1954, he left New Orleans and moved to California. That same year he was employed by Disneyland and played his guitar and banjo on their "river-

Elizabeth Cotton, who wrote the classic "Freight Train," played both the banjo and the guitar. Here, she is in the recording studio cutting a record.

boat" with "The Young Men from New Orleans."**140** Longtime friend and bandleader Kid Ory who worked with St. Cyr in the 1920s said, "He was a fine musician, he knew his music, and he could swing. His banjo used to take the place of the piano in the real old days." Flora, St. Cyr's third wife, said, "He always thought of music. He and his friends got together every Thursday night in the dining room to play the old songs."**141** Johnny St. Cyr died on June 18, 1966.

Elizabeth Cotton (1893–1988)

Elizabeth Cotton was born in Chapel Hill, North Carolina in 1893. She was the youngest of five children. She began playing the banjo at an early age, and by the time she was eleven, she had written a song that was to become her signature piece, "Freight Train."

Elizabeth played both the banjo and guitar upside down. When she was young, her brother owned a banjo. When he was not around, she played it. Because she was left-handed and the banjo was set up for a right-handed player, she played it upside down instead of re-stringing the instrument.

She bought her first guitar when she was twelve, around 1905. She found a job as a maid with a local white family starting at seventy-five cents a month to save for a guitar. Later, they gave her a twenty-five cent raise.

Elizabeth was married at the age of fifteen and, as a result of that and becoming a Christian, she abandoned the banjo and guitar. When her mother died, she moved to Washington, D.C. and began working at Landsburgh's department store. The story goes that during a visit to the store, she helped Ruth Crawford Seeger, whose husband was a musicologist, find her two children, Mike and Peggy. As a result, she struck up a friendship with Ruth and was offered a job working in their household as a domestic.

The Seeger household was surrounded by music and instruments were everywhere. One day while the family was out, Elizabeth picked up one of the

At age 84, Cotton was still entertaining people.

guitars and began to play it. Not realizing the family had returned, she continued to play. The children, upon hearing her, were surprised to learn that she
could play. After that, they invited her to play whenever she wanted to. She
worked for the family for ten years and then, at the age of sixty, began a new
career as a musician. She went on the road with young Mike Seeger and played
with the "New Lost City Rambles."

By her own admission, she only knew a few songs on the banjo. As the times
changed and the guitar became more of an accepted instrument she used it
exclusively. She also incorporated religious music in her repertoire. It is signifi-

cant that for over fifty years Elizabeth did not play the banjo or guitar and then returned to it once the responsibilities of raising a family, earning a living, and being a good Christian did not prevent her from enjoying the banjo and the music she played on it.

At the age of ninety she made a national tour and received a National Heritage Fellowship from the National Endowment for the Arts (1984). She was honored by the Schomberg Center for African-American Research and also won a Grammy in 1985. She died on June 29, 1987 while undergoing surgery for brain seizures. In June of 1998 her guitar was donated to the Smithsonian and is now in the Institution's musical instrument collection.

Conclusion

The banjo players discussed in this book are just a few of the hundreds of African-Americans who made the banjo a part of their lives. Through three centuries in the United States, the banjo has been a part of the evolution of the African-American community from slavery to freedom and beyond. From African storytellers and musicians (griots) to present-day musicians, the banjo remains a symbol of the fusion that took place between the African and European cultures of the United States.

The banjo continues to be a part of the life of our nation. It reminds us of a simpler time when singing off key was okay. A time when the three chords we played over and over again to express our longings, hopes, or fears, were enough. No virtuoso musicians or dulcet-toned vocalists were needed—just a time, a place, and the need to share.

That simple act: playing for the fun and joy of it, is when the banjo is at its best, and why it still sits in the corners of homes all over the world waiting to remind us of who we are and from whence we sprang.

African-American banjo players, like African griots, made significant contributions to the culture of our nation. I agree with Cecelia Conway, "They offered personal expression and communication among the community; social rituals enacted through song and dance; celebrations of the past, clarifications of hardships, of challenges and of identity, performed affecting mediations and eased social pain." [142]

In other words they said what others felt but couldn't say. They expressed their opinions in ways that those who listened needed to hear. And when they performed, whether we danced or sang along, they made us all feel better.

African-Americans say we are the "keepers of the people's memory." One can argue that the banjo has "kept the African-American's memory" as well. It was, and is, a significant part of the African and African-American experience. If we are to fully understand contemporary expressions of African-American culture, particularly as it is expressed through music, the banjo and its legacy must be acknowledged.

Discography

1. *A Treasury of Library of Congress Field Recordings,* Rounder CD 1500.

2. *Banjo Songs, Ballads, and Reels from the Southern Mountains,* Southern Journey Series, Prestige International INT-DS 25004.

3. *Black Banjo Songsters of North Carolina and Virginia,* Smithsonian Folkways SF CD 40079.

4. *Blue Eyed Monster,* Otis Taylor, (Shoelace) CD OT332.

5. *Cannon's Jug Stompers,* Herwin 208.

6. *Early Ellington, 1926-1931,* Decca 3CD 640.

7. *Elizabeth Cotton: Freight Train and Other North Carolina Folk Songs and Tunes,* 33⅓ RPM phonodisc and notes.

8. *Masters of the Banjo*, Arhoolie, CD 421.

9. *Mike Seeger: Southern Banjo Sounds*, Smithsonian Folkways, SFW CD 40107.

10. *Non-Blues Secular Black Music*, Virginia Traditions BRI001.

11. *Smithsonian Folkways American Roots Collection*, Smithsonian Folkways SF CD 40062.

12. *Songs of the Civil War*, New World CD 80202.

13. *Swing Time-Fabulous Big Band Era* 1925-1955, Columbia 3CD 52862.

14. *Taj Mahal/An Evening of Acoustic Music*, Ruff CD 1009.

15. *Taj Mahal/Giant Step*, Columbia CD CGK18.

16. *The Complete Hot Five and Hot Seven Recordings*, Louis Armstrong, Columbia/Legacy CD 2000.

17. *The Early Minstrel Show*, New World CD 80338.

18. *The Harry Smith Collection: A Live Tribute to the Anthology of American Folk Music*, Smithsonian Folkways SFW 40085.

19. *The North Carolina Banjo Collection*, Rounder CD 0439140.

20. *When Negroes Walked the Earth*, Shoelace CD OT333.

Bibliography

Cockrell, Dale. *Demons of Disorder: The Early Blackface Minstrels and Their World.* New York: Cambridge University Press, 1997.

Conway, Cecelia. *African Echoes in Appalachia: A Study of Folk Traditions.* Knoxville: University of Tennessee Press, 1995.

Ellington, Duke. *Music Is My Mistress.* New York: Da Capo Press, 1973.

Epstein, Dena J. "The Folk Banjo: A Documentary History." *Ethnomusicology* 19 (September, 1975): 347-390.

Franklin, John Hope. *From Slavery to Freedom: A History of African Americans.* Eighth Edition. New York: Afred A. Knopf, 2000.

Gura, Phillip F. and James F. Bollman. *America's Instrument: The Banjo in the Nineteenth Century.* Chapel Hill: The University of North Carolina Press, 1999.

Hasse, John Edward, ed. *Ragtime: Its History, Composers, and Music.* New York: Schirmer Books, 1985.

Linn, Karen S. *That Half-Barbaric Twang: The Banjo in American Popular Culture.* Urbana: University of Illinois Press, 1991.

Lott, Eric. *Love and Theft: Blackface Minstrelsy and the American Working Class.* New York: Oxford University Press, 1995.

Milnes, Gerald. *Play of a Fiddle: Traditional Music, Dance, and Folklore in West Virginia.* Lexington: The University Press of Kentucky, 1999.

Nicholson, Stuart. *Reminiscing in Tempo: A Portrait of Duke Ellington.* Boston: Northeastern University Press, 1999.

Northup, Solomon. *Twelve Years a Slave: The Narrative of Solomon Northup.* New York: Derby and Miller, 1853.

Perdue, Charles L., Jr., Thomas E. Barden, Robert K., eds. *Weevils in the Wheat: Interviews with Virginia Ex-Slaves.* Bloomington: Indiana University Press, 1976.

Riis, Thomas L. *Just Before Jazz: Black Musical Theater in New York, 1890 to 1915.* Washington, D.C.: Smithsonian Institution Press, 1989.

Sacks, Howard L., and Judith Rose Sacks. *Way Up North in Dixie: A Black Family's Claim to the Confederate Anthem.* Washington, D.C.: Smithsonian Institution Press, 1993.

Sinful Tunes and Spirituals: Black Folk Music to the Civil War. Urbana: University of Illinois Press, 1977.

Toll, Robert C. *Blacking Up: The Minstrel Show in Nineteenth-Century America.* New York: Oxford University Press, 1974.

Web Sites

Note: All web sites were verified at the time that this book was written. However, web sites may change or become obsolete.

1. *http://www.standingstones.com/banjo.html*
   Brief History of the Banjo

2. *http://www.clarksdale.com/dbm*
   Delta Blues Museum

3. *http://www.rockhall.com/hof*
   Rock and Roll Hall of Fame and Museum

4. *http://www.memphisrocknsoul.org/*
   Memphis Rock 'n Soul Museum

5. *http://www.tulane.edu/~lmiller/OralHistoryIntroduction.html*
   Hogan Jazz Archives

6. *http://www.liunet.edu/cwis/cwp/library/aavaahp.htm*
   African-Americans and the Visual Arts

7. *http://www.liunet.edu/cwis/cwp/library/aavaahp.htm*
   Recordings of African-Americans during Early Ragtime

8. *http://www.gnofn.org/~nopl/exhibits/black96.htm*
   African-Americans in New Orleans

9. *http://www.encarta.msn.com/events/black_history_month/encarta/0CCD2000.asp*
   Encarta Africana online

10. *http://ccharity.com/lynched/georgialynched.htm*
    African-American Lynching since 1859

11. *http://www.jazzportugal.net/escritos_e_entrevistas/escritos/the_loud_music_of_life.html*
    A Brief History of Early Jazz

12. *http://www.chs.org/afamcoll/mss.htm*
    African-American Resources at the Connecticut Historical Society

13. *http://www.weeklywire.com/ww/09-02-97/nash_cover.html*
    The Nashville Scene and African-American Music

14. *http://web2.si.edu/folkways/40108notes.htm*
    Doc Boggs and Early African-American Folk Music

15. *http://www.philly.com/packages/history/news/quiz020200.asp*
    A Black History Test

16. *http://www.arbooks.com/pmh.htm*
    Popular Music History and Reference

17. *http://www.teleport.com/~repmail/af-am-mu.html*
    Essay about African-American Music Commissioned by Portland School System.

18. *http://www.the-forum.com/globalvillage/afamtrad.htm*
    African-American Music Traditions

19. *http://books.philly.com/chapter/nonfict/gioia_t01.asp*
African-American Banjo Music and History of Jazz

20. *http://lcweb2.loc.gov/ammem/ndlpedu/book/a.html*
Library of Congress Resources

21. *http://www.virginia.edu/~vafolk/ffv1.htm*
Folklife and Folklore in Virginia

22. *http://www.saltdal.vgs.no/prosjekt/slavrute/elever/musikk/music1.htm*
Slave Trade and Its Influence on African-American Music

23. *http://www.undergroundrailroad.org/history/africans3.html*
African Roots of American Culture

24. *http://www.courses.dsu.edu/eled360/publish/donnan.htm#dnMusic*
Educational Units on African-American History, Fourth Grade Level

25. *http://www.uni-paderborn.de/~pg/kunda.html*
Griots of West Africa

26. *http://lcweb.loc.gov/rr/mopic/jazz/d-f.html*
A Guide to Jazz in Film

27. *http://www.fwkc.com/encyclopedia/low/articles/j/j013000287f.html*
A History of Jazz

28. *http://jambands.com/apr00/features/blueground.html*
Article on Banjo and Folk Music

29. *http://www3.sympatico.ca/villagejazz/RESPECT.HTM*
Jazz and the Banjo

30. *http://www2.ios.com/~zepp29/banjbib.htm*
A Bibliography of the Banjo

Glossary

banjar, banger, bangeon, bangelo, strum strum, merrywang—various names referring to the banjo.

banjoist—a professional banjo player.

black intelligencia—Educated African-Americans who were part of an intellectual elite during the first half of the twentieth century.

blackface—the process of smearing burnt cork or black shoe polish on one's face to portray African-Americans who were enslaved.

burnt cork—substance used to blacken the face. Used by minstrels primarily during the nineteenth century.

carpetbagger—a Northerner who went to the South during the Reconstruction period to seek political office or to take advantage of the political or social disruption during the aftermath of the Civil War.

cash crop—agricultural crops raised specifically for the ability to make money (i.e. cotton, tobacco, soybeans, etc.)

craps—a game in which two dice are thrown and in which a throw of 7 or 11 wins and a first throw of two, three, or twelve loses. A first throw of four, five, six, eight, nine, or ten can be won only by repeating the number thrown before a seven appears.

darky—derogatory term for an uncultured, uneducated rural African-American during the nineteenth and early twentieth centuries.

delineator—term used when referring to performers and actors known for their ability to portray others.

democratic ideal—the belief that political and social equality should be enjoyed by all.

domestic crop—crops raised as basic stables, to feed the farmer and his family (i.e. corn, green beans, tomatoes, potatoes, etc.).

field hollar—worksongs sung by enslaved African-Americans while working as farm and plantation laborers.

folk music—music created in informal settings by musicians with little or no formal training.

griot—French-derived term for African storyteller/musicians who lived in, and around, Senegal, West Africa.

halam—one of a family of lute-type stringed instruments from the Senegambia region of West Africa believed to be the ancestor of the banjo.

highbrow—a person of superior intellect, class, interests, and tastes.

Jim Crow—a practice of discriminating against African-Americans and segregating them in public facilities, public vehicles, education, and other public accommodations during the late nineteenth and early twentieth centuries.

About the Author

Biography

D r. Rex Ellis has been a storyteller for twenty years. His interest in storytelling began while working at the Colonial Williamsburg Foundation, in Williamsburg, Virginia. While there he used storytelling as a means of teaching African-American history. His specialties include folk culture, slavery, music, and African-American history.

He uses storytelling in every aspect of his work, both as a museum educator, historian, and sought-after consultant to museums throughout the country. He has taken his craft to Johannesburg, South Africa, Ponce, Puerto Rico, Panama, Quebec, Toronto, St. Croix, St. Thomas, New Zealand, British Columbia, as well as countless festivals, schools, museums, and special events throughout the United States.

He is presently chair/curator in the Division of Cultural History at the National Museum of American History, at the Smithsonian Institution. Prior to coming to the Smithsonian, Dr. Ellis directed the Department of African-American Interpretation and Presentations at the Colonial Williamsburg Foundation in Williamsburg, Virginia.

Dr. Ellis received his Bachelor of Fine Arts from Virginia Commonwealth University, a Masters from Wayne State University, and his doctorate in Higher Education from the College of William and Mary. He has contributed articles to such publications as *The Colonial Williamsburg Journal, American Visions,* and *History News.* He has memberships in the Screen Actor's Guild, American Federation of Television and Radio Artists, the American Association of Museums, American Association for State and Local History, the Association of Black Storytellers, and the National Storytelling Association.

As a professional storyteller, he has conducted workshops and consultancies at a variety of educational institutions, focusing on teaching history through storytelling. His work is featured in *African-American Folktales: For Young Readers,* published by August House, *The Storyteller's Start-up Book* by Margaret Read MacDonald, *Tales as Tools: Complete Guide to Storytelling in the Classroom,* and *Jump Up and Say,* a new anthology of stories by Linda and Clay Goss. His most recent book, *Beneath the Blazing Sun,* was published by August House in 1997.

Of the power of storytelling, Dr. Ellis says:

I truly believe that the power of storytelling is the one best hope we have to improve the communities we live in and the people we love. I have seen people with different backgrounds talk to each other for the first time. I have seen fathers, mothers, sons and daughters who seldom speak to each other laughing, reminiscing, and reconnecting because of storytelling. I have seen inner-city kids, who have decided to leave their guns at home, express the stories they so desperately need to tell with pencils and paper instead. I have seen bridges built with storytelling that invite listeners and tellers to unite in ways that are more potent than a town meeting and more healing than a therapy session. It is pretty hard to hate someone whose story you know.

Personal

My life has been one big journey, based on my belief that Americans talk more about each other than to each other. We spend a great deal of time segregating ourselves from each other, assuming that our own individual way of life is the best, our culture is the best, our way of thinking is the best, our color is the best, and our community is the best. I have always tried to use my stories as a means to build bridges. I 'd rather be a part of the solution than a part of the problem. If we don't learn to live together, it won't be because I'm not out there every chance I get, suggesting that we have more in common as a people than we think we do. If this book makes a contribution to that cause, then it will have been worth the effort.

I am more driven by what I don't know than by what I do know. If there are any successes in my life, it is because I have never stopped learning and discovering. I'm just smart enough to realize how dumb I am.

Growing up as an African-American in the United States has been a roller coaster ride full of emotions and experiences. I hope my work, in some way, will be liberating for other African-Americans and informative to others interested in understanding what the American identity means from where I sit.

Endnotes

1. Cecelia Conway, *African Banjo Echoes in Appalachia: A Study of Folk Traditions* (Knoxville: The University of Tennessee Press, 1995).

2. Performers like Joe and Odell Thompson, John Jackson, Archie Edwards, Dink Roberts, and others had abandoned their banjo roots. Scholars such as Kip Lornell, Cecilia Conway, Scott Odell, Mike Seegar and others saw the significance of the legacy, and convinced these musicians to revive their memories and facilitated performances that have been enjoyed around the world.

3. W.E.B. Du Bois, "Of the Sorrow Songs." In *The Negro in Music and Art* edited by Lindsay Patterson for The Association for the Study of Negro Life and History (New York: Publishers Company, Inc., 1968.), 10.

4. Elizabeth Baroody, "Banjo, the Sound of America." *Early American Life* vol. 7, n. 2 (April 1976), 57.

5. A 1787 report stated that a Virginia Negro kept "time and cadence, most exactly, with the music of the banjo." In "Manner of Living of the Inhabitants of Virginia," *The American Museum* vol. I, n. 3 (March 1787), 2nd ed., 214–216.

6. According to Schreyer, there is little doubt that, "the banjo was the middle passage through which rhythms of black music came to the piano." *The Banjo in Ragtime,* 54.

7. Sue Eakin and Joseph Logsdon, eds., *Twelve Years a Slave: By Solomon Northup.* (Baton Rouge: Louisiana State University Press, 1968), 165–66.

8. Schreyer, *The Banjo in Ragtime,* 54.

9. For more on the African origins of the banjo, see Cecelia C. Conway's book *African Banjo Echoes in Appalachia: A Study of Folk Traditions* (Knoxville: University of Tennessee Press, 1995).

10. Michael Coolen, "The Fodet: A Senegambian Origin for the Blues?" *The Black Perspective in Music.* vol. 10, n. 1, Spring 1982, 73–75.

11. Conway, 27.

12. There is some debate as to whether the halam was used by griots or in fact by musicians or nobles who also composed music. A three-stringed instrument called the Konting Saba is mentioned in Senegal as the instrument that was popular among griots and jolis. Also see Conway, 28.

13. See Conway, p. 27. Wayne Shrubsall's program notes in *Masters of the Banjo.* Produced by the National Council for the Traditional Arts, 1994, p. 4. See also Coolen, pp. 72, 73, and Robert Winans, *The Banjo: From Africa to Virginia and Beyond.* "Blue Ridge Folk Instruments and Their Makers," an exhibit catalogue organized by the Blue Ridge Institute of Ferrum College, Ferrum, Virginia, 19.

14. Musician Patrick Davis traveled to Senegal in 1997 and brought back this information gathered from Senegalese scholars and musicians.

15. Michael Gomez, *Exchanging Our Country Marks: The Transformation of African Identities in the Colonial and Antebellum South* (Chapel Hill: University of North Carolina Press, 1998), 45. A recent paper written by Ulf Jagfors, a banjo collector in Sweden, indicates new evidence that the banjo's origins may also be linked to Gambia. The paper, which was presented to the third annual Banjo Collectors meeting in Boston in November 2000, indicates a connection to the banjo, the Jola community, and a lute-styled instrument called the Akonting.

16. Michael Coolen, "The Fodet: A Senegambian Origin for the Blues?" *The Black Perspective in Music.* The Foundation for Research in the Afro-American Creative Arts Inc., Post Office Drawer I, Cambria Heights, New York, 1982, 72.

17. Dena Epstein, *Sinful Tunes and Spirituals* (Chicago: University of Chicago Press, 1977), 5.

18. Ibid.

19. Stanley Sadie, ed., *The New Grove Dictionary of American Music* (New York: Macmillan, 1995), 119.

20. From the *Journal of Nicholas Creswell* from Nanjemoy, Maryland, Sunday, May 29th, 1774, 18–19.

21. Thomas Jefferson, *Notes on the State of Virginia*, 257.

22. Call and response type of singing that initially incorporated a leader reciting words of a psalm and the chorus or congregation repeating the verse or refrain as instructed. The psalms of the bible, which were the first religious words to be put to music, were sung by a leader who would establish the pitch and tune, and would sing loudly and clearly enough to be heard by all. Africans and African-Americans picked up this European tradition. Eventually tunes were altered and embellished, and in this way, folksongs and improvisational singing grew. This method of singing allowed unlettered blacks to sing as a group and use biblical text. See Eileen Southern, *The Music of Black Americans*, 31.

23. Southern, on page 81, says, that "Crooked Shanks" was "attributed to a composer named Gardner and may be one of his 'large number of tunes' that was popular with amateurs of his time."

24. Epstein, 30.

25. Edward Long, *History of Jamaica*, II, 423.

26. Epstein, 36.

27. Epstein, 85.

28. Epstein, 138.

29. Creswell, *Journal*, 19, entry of May 29, 1774, Nanjemoy, Maryland.

30. Boucher, *Glossary*, BAN.

31. Eileen Southern, *The Music of Black Americans: A History* (New York: W.W. Norton & Company, 1971), 151.

32. Karen Linn, *That Half-Barbaric Twang: The Banjo in American Popular Culture* (Chicago: University of Illinois Press, 1991), 42.

33. For additional information on the spiritual and its personal expression, see *The International Library of Negro Life and History: The Negro in Music and Art.* Edited by Lindsay Patterson. Published under the auspices of The Association for the Study of Negro Life and History (New York: Publishers Company. Inc., 1968), 15.

34. Linn, 43.

35. John Hope Franklin, *From Slavery to Freedom: A History of Negro Americans* (New York: Alfred A. Knopf, 1980), 102.

36. Southern, 103.

37. See Ira Berlin, *Many Thousands Gone: The First Two Centuries of Slavery in North America* (Cambridge: The Belknap Press of Harvard University Press, 1998), 308–309.

38. Alexander Saxton, "Black face Minstrelsy and the Jacksonian Ideology," *American Quarterly,* vol. 27, 1975, 5.

39. Matthews, 755.

40. Harry A. Ploski and Warren Marr II., eds., *The Negro Almanac: A Reference Work on the Afro-American* (New York: Bellwether Publishing, 1976), 807.

41. "Documentary Evidence," *Mississippi in 1875,* Senate Report 527, Part II, 44th Congress, First Session (Washington, 1876), 19–56.

42. Franklin, 263.

43. Robert C. Toll, *Blacking Up: The Minstrel Show in Nineteenth-Century America* (New York: Oxford University Press, 1974), 34.

44. Larence Hutton, "The Negro on the Stage," *Harper's New Monthly Magazine,* 140.

45. Ibid., 141.

46. Saxton, 4.

47. Ibid., 17.

48. Matthews, 755. Also see Howard Sackler, *Way Up North in Dixie,* for a convincing argument regarding the authorship of "Dixie."

49. Ibid., 18.

50. Ibid.

51. Christy's *Plantation Melodies No. 2* (Philadelphia: Fisher, 1853), 35.

52. *Christy's Ram's Horn Nigga Songster* (New York: Marsh, n.d.), 102.

53. Arthur Woodward, "Joel Sweeney and the First Banjo," *Los Angeles County Museum Quarterly.* Spring, 1949, vols. 3, 7, 8.

54. Ibid., 10.

55. His brother Dick, who was two years younger than Joel, died in 1860 and is buried in Washington, D.C.

56. Samuel D. Sweeney was listed as a private on the roster of Co. H, 2nd Virginia Cavalry. The same source also notes that he was a great banjo player, and that he died of smallpox at Hanover Court House. H.B. McClellan in the *The Campaigns. Of Stuart's Calvary*, 440.

57. Lieutenant Colonel W.W. Blackford, of Jeb Stuart's staff, mentions Sweeney several times in his memoirs, *War Years with Jeb Stuart* (Charles Scribner's and Sons, 1945).

58. *Los Angeles Quarterly*, 10.

59. Frank Converse, "Old Cremora," *Songster* (New York: Dick, 1863), 9–10.

60. Virginia Adam, ed., *On the Altar of Freedom: A Black Soldier's Civil War Letters from the Front* (Amherst: The University of Massachusetts Press, 1991), 39.

61. Walter Dean Myers, *Now Is Your Time: The African American Struggle for Freedom* (New York: HarperTrophy, 1991), 233.

62. Ibid.

63. Southern, 93.

64. W.E.B. Du Bois stated, "The Negro race, like all races, is going to be saved by its exceptional men. The problem of education, then, among Negroes must first of all deal with the Talented Tenth; it is the problem of developing the Best of this race that they may guide the Mass away from the contamination and death of the Worst, in their own and other races." Found in *Black Protest Thought in the Twentieth Century*, edited by August Meier, Elliott Rudwick and Francis L. Broderick (New York: The Bobbs-Merrill Company, Inc., 1971), 48.

65. Linn, 57.

66. Ibid., 58.

67. Ibid., 65.

68. James B. Fry, *New York and the Conscription Act of 1863: A Chapter in the History of the Civil War* (New York: Putnam, 1885).

69. John Hope Franklin, p. 213. See also Middleton Harris, et al., *The Black Book* (New York: Random House, 1974), 72.

70. Patterson, "Of the Sorrow Songs," 10.

71. Gerald Milnes, *Play of a Fiddle: Traditional Music, Dance, and Folklore in West Virginia* (Lexington: The University Press of Kentucky, 1999), 21.

72. R.C. Toll, *Blacking Up,* 223.

73. Ibid., 227.

74. Ibid., 46–50.

75. W.C. Handy, *Father of the Blues* (New York, 1941, Collier ed.), 36.

76. Toll, 248–250.

77. Alain Locke, "The Age of Minstrelsy," *Negro in Music and Art: The International Library of Negro Life and History* (New York: The Association for the Study of Negro Live and History, 1968), 38.

78. Toll, 221.

79. Portions of text excerpted from *Lynching in the New South: Georgia and Virginia 1880–1930* (Urbana: University of Illinois Press, 1993) by W. Fitzhugh Brundage.

80. Ibid., 275–280.

81. For more information about lynching, see the following:

   • National Association for the Advancement of Colored People, *Thirty Years of Lynching in the United States*, 1889–1918 (New York: Arno Press, 1969).

   • Walter Francis White, *Rope and Faggot* (New York: Arno Press, 1969).

   • Jacquelyn Dowd Hall, *Revolt Agaist Chivalry: Jessie Daniel Ames and the Women's Campaign Against Lynching* (New York: Columbia University Press, 1979).

   • George C. Wright, *Racial Violence in Kentucky, 1865–1940: Lynchings, Mob Rule, and "Legal Lynchings"* (Baton Rouge: Louisiana State University Press, 1990).

   • Ida B. Wells-Barnett, *On Lynchings: Southern Horrors, A Red Record, Mob Rule in New Orleans* (Salem, New Hampshire: Ayer Co., 1991).

   • Arthur Franklin Raper, *The Tragedy of Lynching* (New York: Negro University Press, 1969).

82. See Linn's *That Half Barbaric Twang.*

83. Charles L. Perdue, Jr., Thomas E. Barden and Robert K. Phillips, eds., *Weevils in the Wheat: Interviews with Virginia Ex-Slaves* (Charlottesville: University of Virginia Press, 1976), 49.

84. Ibid., 267.

85. Perdue, 316.

86. Eileen Southern, 279.

87. Ibid., 281.

88. Ibid., 282.

89. Ibid., 300.

90. John Edward Hasse, ed., *Ragtime: Its History, Composers, and Music* (New York: Schirmer Books, 1985), 90–91.

91. Alyn Shipton, "Banjo," *The New Grove Dictionary of Jazz* (New York: St. Martin's Press, 1994), 65.

92. Ibid.

93. Ibid., 66.

94. Southern, 337.

95. Linn, 44.

96. Ibid., 67.

97. Barry Kernfeld, ed., *The New Grove Dictionary of Jazz* (New York: St. Martin's Press, 1994), 464.

98. *Pennsylvania Gazette,* 7 July 1749, 2 November 1749, and 17 November 1757.

99. It is also possible that Scipio was hired out to work for others for a period of time and simply didn't like where he was and left to get back to Philadelphia. Because of this skill as a musician, he was very marketable and useful to anyone who wanted to capitalize on his skills as a musician.

100. Figuring eighty miles from Maryland to Philadelphia and a normal person taking twenty minutes to walk a mile.

101. William B. Smith, "The Persimmon Tree and the Beer Dance." *Farmers' Register,* VI (Shellbanks, VA., April 1838), 58–61.

102. *Pennsylvania Gazette,* 2 November 1749.

103. Ibid.

104. For examples of other banjo players in the colonial period see Epstein's *Sinful Tunes and Spirituals,* the *Journal of Philip Vickers Fithian,* and Eileen Southern's *The Music of Black Americans.*

105. Linn, 45.

106. Ibid., 46.

107. David Ewen, *American Songwriters* (New York: The H.W. Wilson Company, 1987), 53.

108. August Meier, Elliot Rudwick, and Francis L. Broderick, *Black Protest Thought in the Twentieth Century.* Second Edition (New York: The Bobbs-Merrill Company, Inc., 1971), 72.

109. Langston Hughes, *Famous Negro Music Makers.* New York: Dodd Mead, 1957, 31.

110. Dennis Agay, *Best Loved Songs of the American People* (New York: Doubleday, 1975).

111. Ibid., 54.

112. Ibid.

113. H. Wiley Hitchcock and Stanley Sadie, eds., *The New Grove Dictionary of American Music.* Volume One A–D. (London: Macmillan Press Limited, 1986), 231.

114. Quoted from "Famous Men of Flushing: James A. Bland, Prince of the Colored Songwriters" 1944, Charles Maywood, Flushing Historical Society.

115. Quoted in Ewen, 54.

116. Wilkins Lane, *Walk Right In: Based Upon the Life and Times of Gus Cannon* (Tennessee: Museum Publishing, 1995). (Published by Lane Wilkins) LC 56126090, 29.

117. Ibid., 20.

118. Ibid.

119. Bengt Olsson, "Gus Cannon and Banjo Joe." Biography accompanying the recording. August-September, 1973, 1.

120. Ibid.

121. Wilkins, 48.

122. Olsson, 1.

123. Ibid., 2.

124. Wilkins, 56.

125. Olsson, 4.

126. Ibid., 2.

127. Ibid., 4.

128. Wilkins, 76.

129. Olsson, 4.

130. More information about Gus Cannon can be found at the Delta Blues Museum in Clarksdale, Mississippi.

131. Hogan Jazz Archive, Howard-Tilton Memorial Library, Tulane University. Oral history transcription of Johnny St. Cyr, with William Russell and Manuel Manetta, August, 27, 1958, 6.

132. Johnny St. Cyr, "Jazz as I Remember It." Part Three: *The Riverboats.* Oral history transcribed by John W. Slingsby. From vertical file information on Johnny St. Cyr, Hogan Jazz Archive, Tulane University, 6.

133. Ibid., 9.

134. Epstein, 134.

135. St. Cyr oral history, 7.

136. "Jazz as I remember It,"6.

137. The quadrille is a French dance that was popular in New Orleans during the nineteenth century. It is thought to have influenced the dances done during the ragtime era. The dance had a particular meter that alternated from 6/8 time to 2/4 time. For more information see Tilford Brooks, *America's Black Musical Heritage*, 70.

138. "Jazz as I remember It," 23.

139. Ibid., 8.

140. Obituary of Johnny St. Cyr. *New Orleans Times Picayune*, June 18, 1966.

141. Ibid.

142. Conway, 286.